Dear Ross and Noreen,

Congratulations on your engagement! We hope that this book will be helpful in your preparations for marriage and the rest of your life.

God Bless You

Love
Bill & Carol

Tenderness
and 24 Other Ways to Make a Marriage Work

Tenderness
and 24 Other Ways to Make a Marriage Work

❦

Nelson Price

Fleming H. Revell Company
Old Tappan, New Jersey

Unless otherwise identified, Scripture quotations are from the King James Version of the Bible.

The Scripture quotations contained herein identified RSV are from the Revised Standard Version of the Bible, Copyrighted © 1946, 1952, 1971, by the Division of Christian Education of the National Council of the Churches of Christ in the United States of America, and are used by permission. All rights reserved.

Scripture quotations identified NEB are from The New English Bible. Copyright © The Delegates of the Oxford University Press and the Syndics of the Cambridge University Press 1961, 1970. Reprinted by permission.

"Non-Stop" from LOVE POEMS FOR THE VERY MARRIED by Lois Peters (Thomas Y. Crowell)
Copyright © 1967 by Lois Wyse
Reprinted by permission of Harper & Row, Publishers, Inc.

Library of Congress Cataloging-in-Publication Data

Price Nelson L.
   Tenderness and 24 other ways to make a marriage work.

   1. Marriage. 2. Marriage—Religious aspects—Christianity. 3. Communication in marriage. I. Title.
II. Title: Tenderness and twenty-four other ways to make a marriage work.
HQ734.P919   1986   646.7′8   85-29677
ISBN 0-8007-1471-7

Copyright © 1986 by Nelson Price
All rights reserved
Printed in the United States of America
Published by the Fleming H. Revell Company
Old Tappan, NJ 07675

Contents

	Introduction	7
	1. Leaving and Cleaving	11
	2. The Plan for Man and Woman	27
	3. How to Be a Winning Wife	36
	4. How to Be a Huggable Husband	50
	5. Love Her, Lover	68
	6. The Cost of Communicating	81
	7. You Determine Your Attitude	92
	8. Know the Troubled Waters	100

9.
Traits of a Good Relationship — 115

10.
Tenderness and 24 Other Ways to
Make a Marriage Work — 129

11.
Got a Problem? Got Five Minutes?
Read This! — 153

Introduction

Your marriage can never be as good as it once was—it can be *better* than it ever was. That may sound impossible, but it is true. Regardless of how sick or how healthy your marriage is, it can be even more gratifying, fulfilling, and rewarding. I feel confident in that for two reasons.

One is that the biblical basis for marriage guarantees it. The divine design is intended to utilize the maximum potential of both parties to the fullest. God's plan for marriage will work for you.

Furthermore, I am confident your marriage can be better than it ever was because I have seen it happen. As a pastor, I have engaged in a great deal of marriage counseling. Over a span of more than twenty years, I have counseled thousands of couples. Such experience prompts me to believe there is no marriage that can't succeed—and none that can't fail. The outcome depends on the input. I have watched couples who felt they had a good marriage become complacent about their commitment, and as a result their relationship atrophied. I have counseled numerous couples who have gone so far as to file for divorce. Even then, those who expressed a willingness to employ the divine plan for marriage and worked at it found that their marriage could be maximized.

After a stormy six years of unhappy marriage, Ralph and Beth divorced. At this late stage they expressed a desire to try applying the basic standards of Scripture in a new life together. Their remarriage has proven to be much better than any phase of their previous marriage.

This example is shared in the hope that even the most defeated of couples will not give up on their marriage. It *can* work. The principles herein not only have been tried and proven, but they have the authority of heaven behind them. God is as good as His Word. His Word is as good as He.

Human beings are creatures of change. The fact that a good marriage might have gone bad indicates a negative change has occurred. Positive change takes patience, perseverance, and practice. Enduring intent can make constructive change happen. Reliance on God as builder or rebuilder of your marriage results in a right and rewarding relationship. "Except the Lord build the house, they labour in vain that build it . . ." (Psalms 127:1).

This book is written to encourage you and instill faith in you that the best for your marriage is yet to come. Hoping the best will come is closely connected to your willingness to take the initiative in making it come. If you have tried your way, or before you do, try God's way. He has a plan for your marriage.

Tenderness
and 24 Other Ways to Make a Marriage Work

1

Leaving and Cleaving

You see marriage differently when your child marries. Sharon and I were very close; a beautiful bond existed between us as father and daughter. In this relationship we had shared the joys and sorrows of her growth to adulthood.

A few weeks earlier, she had stood beside her striking groom as I pronounced them husband and wife—Mr. and Mrs. Randy Turner. It was an emotional, joyous moment. Having given her away, I had then joined them together.

Now, only a few weeks later, the two of them were visiting Cairo, Egypt, with us. We had had a long night in airports in Frankfurt and Amman before we arrived in Cairo at 5:00 A.M.

The tour began punctually at 8:00 A.M. Our first stop was

the great pyramids. Suffering from jet lag, Sharon initially decided to stay on the bus, since she had visited the pyramids twice before.

Randy and I had worked our way through the crowded camel lot and were about to mount when we heard Sharon's familiar voice calling out from the other side of the milling mob. There was a note of fear in it. She had decided to join us, and now the shouting of guides and bellowing of camels nearly drowned out her voice. Flowing robes and colorful saddles blocked our vision. At the point of panic, with her life literally in danger, she called out once more. The direction from which her voice came let us know she was in the middle of the camel-lot melee. I started to run to meet her, then it dawned on me—she was calling Randy, not Daddy. I stopped, he continued to rush toward her, and I watched as they met in a sweeping, comforting embrace.

Momentarily my heart sank. This child I loved so much, whom I had consoled for years, now found her comfort and security in the arms of another. My role as father had to yield to Randy's role as husband.

Then instinctively I said to myself, "Good-bye, Sharon. Hello, Mrs. Turner." In Sharon's moment of panic and Randy's embrace, I understood what the words of the marriage ceremony meant: leave and cleave.

Parents have to yield their bond. Parties engaging in marriage have to yearn to bond.

Long before there were in-laws, God in His wisdom instructed couples to leave father and mother and cleave to each other. This was done at a time when there were only two people on earth. Divine insight foresaw the potential problems that might result if either element were taken lightly. Both leaving and cleaving must be absolute. One complements the other.

Leaving

Ron and Julie married young. His wealthy parents lovingly offered them one floor of their beautiful, spacious home as a temporary residence. The four truly loved one another. Because they enjoyed being together and for economic reasons, they ate two meals a day together. Their church, social, and work careers merged as one. Everything they did was together. Soon that became a factor driving Ron and Julie apart.

Relief was in sight. Ron's dad, a builder, had promised them a new house from the start. After a year together, the house was nearly complete. They took heart over being able to establish their own independent life. One month before its completion, Ron's dad announced he had such a good offer on the house, he sold it. After all, he said, "I'll be opening another subdivision in less than a year."

Now depression was added to their distress. Ron was torn between two women—his mother and his wife; Julie between two men—her husband and her father-in-law.

Ron's loving, sweet-spirited parents were only beginning to note that the four-party living arrangement they were enjoying so much was imposing on Ron and Julie. Tensions grew. Conflicts among the four people who loved one another increased.

In heartbreak, Ron and Julie visited me late one night, seeking help for their floundering marriage. Only now could they admit to themselves the pressure created by their lack of privacy.

After discussing a strategy for the two of them to use in talking it out with the involved parents, they left feeling hopeful. What followed is a tribute to loving understanding. The proposed new house was moved up as a priority on the construction charts, and the anticipation of independence increased everyone's tolerance. The move was made, and the four of them now live happily, cleaving two-by-two. This was made possible by two leaving.

Parents not only have to let their children go—they must aid the departure. This is contrary to all other forms of love. As a child yourself, you wanted to possess and provide for the object of your love. A toy, pet, or doll that was yours was the object of your all-consuming desire. You wanted to keep it.

Parenthood is the only role in life in which the object of our love is reared to be given away.

Remember at the altar the question was posed, "Who *gives* this woman to be joined in holy matrimony?"

Parents must unhesitatingly give away the object of their love. Experiencing difficulty in doing it must not keep it from being done. Some things are easier to say than to do, but they must be done when right.

The child must also realize the imperatives of leaving. Leaving is not a disavowal of love or a hint of a decline in regard. Leaving only acknowledges the establishment of a new base of authority, a new primacy of allegiance, a new center of devotion.

Even if geographic proximity remains, there must be a separation. The new couple must establish their own friends, schedules, and routines. They must have their own privacy. Intrusion by well-intended in-laws can be very detrimental. Openness and understanding cause people to forget about the possibility of hurt feelings when the priority of love prevails.

When Gail and Tony moved to Atlanta, she left behind the security of a loving family in a small rural community. The adjustments of marriage, coupled with cultural shock, resulted in homesickness for Gail. Anyone having suffered from this strong emotion knows her pain. She pined for her parents and longed for her forfeited friendships.

Instinctively, Tony realized he needed to help her brew a new glue. His understanding attentiveness built her confidence in him. Wisely he initiated their mutual involvement in a vibrant church with a well-rounded program for couples. He encouraged her to visit her former home. Almost imperceptibly, her loyalties started to change—an antidote for homesickness had been found. No love for what was formerly cherished was forfeited, but new interests were developed. Homesickness became an intuitive compliment to the home that had produced her and matured her for not only leaving but cleaving.

Leaving speaks of independence, which is what all parties

involved should strive for. Only when independence exists can there be development into a mature person.

Cleaving

The biblical term *cleave* literally means to be bonded together. It is the equivalent of super glue. Cleaving means to be permanently bonded—no hint of separation is contained. Emphatic permanence is the emphasis. In part, the marriage vow states, " . . . until death do us part." No couple should ever give verbal consent to that while holding mental reservations.

Bond Breakers

There are identifiable, progressive steps that lead to breaking the marriage bond. I have noticed six factors that minimize a marriage. Observation of any one of them should cause caution to be taken to avoid progressing to the next.

Assumption Many couples assume their marriage will always be the greatest. They take for granted that they will grow together and that nothing needs to be done to keep the marriage fresh and alive. They don't deliberately do anything to diminish their marriage, but neither do they do anything to nourish it. They assume it will grow; this is a false assumption. Marriage, like a garden, has to be cultivated. It requires a lifelong plan of cultivation. Marriages go through so many different phases, and success in one phase does not assure success in the next. Constant adjustments have to be made. No "we've got it made" stage exists. The present increase in divorce among older couples indicates there is no safe stage in a marriage where a couple can coast.

Bryon and Lee had three sons, two daughters, and nine grandchildren. He loved to hunt and enjoyed an active social life. She had no outside interests and became a TV soap-opera addict. Her grooming deteriorated. His weight increased. Compliments were never shared. All ties in the marriage were loosened when a threat to their marriage appeared. Having assumed there was no need to continue to cultivate their relationship, it failed after forty years.

Attrition General (and perhaps initially unidentifiable) discontent occurs next. Marriages, like clocks, have a tendency to run down. Some vague dissatisfaction is felt, which at first is not distinguishable. Some unexpected stress may arise, and it then becomes apparent that the strength normally enjoyed in confronting such challenges together is gone. Under normal circumstances this attrition might not be recognized. However, circumstances don't stay normal for long. If attrition is tolerated and not dealt with soon, stress will eventually test the relationship. When it does, questions and doubts emerge. Thoughts such as, "Our marriage might not be all that I thought it was," simmer in the mind. The torturing idea that "Maybe this marriage wasn't made in heaven," flutters through the mind like birds in a spring breeze.

Attention The presence of these unspoken doubts makes it very difficult to concentrate on the many positive aspects of the marriage. Negatives become the focal point. Unfortunately, this causes a person to overlook or be insensitive to the many pluses in the marriage. A negative mind set develops, a critical nature emerges, and complaints begin to be more frequently expressed.

Jane was overheard at a party, running down her husband, Joe. She had a great personality and friends were engulfed in laughter at her description of some of Joe's personal weaknesses. Her one-liners were zinging him, to their delight. The first time Jane did this, everyone thought it was cute. Over the months, it ceased to be funny to Joe's friends. They soon realized it was camouflaged caustic criticism arising from Jane's basically critical spirit.

At this stage there were many good, pleasant, and enjoyable aspects to their marriage that were being frequently

Leaving and Cleaving

overlooked. The negative nature dwelt on little unpleasant things and made them big deals. Suddenly they became critical issues. The marriage got out of focus. One or both parties suffered from poor vision. They were seeing only half of the picture, and it was the wrong half.

There are weaknesses in every marriage. Magnifying them does great damage to the marriage. They must be dealt with, but in light of the positive aspects of the relationship. Failure to do so resulted in Jane and Joe's marriage dissolving.

Aspiration With this frame of mind existing, the imagination runs wild. "I wish I had never gotten into this mess. I wish I had my freedom again."

We do have short memories, don't we? One reason couples gave up their freedom was that it wasn't so hot, either. As a matter of fact, they were pretty discontented with it at one time. That in part motivated them to get married.

Speculation begins at this point. "I wonder what it would be like to be free?" If another attractive offer comes along, the alternative may even become, "I wonder what life would be like with someone else."

When things have deteriorated to this point, the glue is losing its grip. Freedom looks inviting and exciting. Frequently someone other than one's mate may seem to embody all the admirable assets desired in a marriage. This further weakens the marriage bond.

Comparing one's spouse to a rival outside the marriage is not only improper, but impossible. It is like comparing apples and oranges. One's mate represents responsibility, and the other party represents freedom. Most persons have enough latent irresponsibility within that a little stimulus causes it to become dominant.

Remember, back at the altar you said, "Until death do us part." You waived all other options at that point. You then assumed the right to be responsible. You took on a new freedom—the freedom to be dependable, reliable, and committed.

Articulation Until now all of this has been secretive. These covert concepts may have been going on for some time. By the time the ideas are articulated, they may have become desires. A partner is shocked when suddenly a mate says, "I want a divorce." When there has been no discussion, no attempt at resolving issues, it comes as a surprise and shock.

Lou's career had exceeded her expectation. Tom's job had become a demanding mistress. Lou's schedule required her to travel. By the time she got home on weekends, she needed to rest. On the road, fresh and charming, she met someone who showed interest in her. She lied about missed flights and extended weekend work. At home she mastered the hypocritical role of a faithful wife. Never did she hint of discontent. Then one day she dropped the bomb: "I want a divorce." There was no attempt at explaining or resolving their problems. An emphatic "that's it" stunned Tom. She pursued the divorce before he could recover and reason with her. Having stated her new intent, pride became dominant. It was then difficult to change her mind. Having secretly contemplated it for a long time, she now felt obligated to prove her point by pushing for the divorce.

Actualization Divorce is pursued. Review the steps to this final stage. Where are you in your marriage? The trend can be reversed. The marriage can be saved. It can be better than it ever was. In your attitude, move back through the stages to point one, *assumption*.

Don't assume, assert. Assert "I am going to work at doing what I can to make our marriage better, regardless of the response my efforts meet."

Bond Makers

We might call marriage happiness "a consummation devoutly to be wish'd."

That carries us beyond a starry-eyed idealism. It erases any reservation clause or if-it-doesn't-work-out attitude.

"So long as you both shall live" echoes daily in the heart.

To *will* to keep your vows means to avoid all threats to your allegiance. All challenges to your relationship must be dealt with in a positive and constructive manner. Love takes responsibility and asserts initiative in maintaining the bond.

Chemically, most adhesives are compounds. They consist of the proper mix of the right ingredients. Likewise there are certain elements in marriage that provide the right mix for a good bond. Some are:

Fortress Building each other up affords a great sense of fulfillment; others will do a superb job of eroding your vitality. Every person has a God-given ego. Erosion results when you:

    1. Use humor at the expense of your mate.
    2. Embarrass your mate in public.
    3. Fail to defend your mate from undue criticism.
    4. Pass up opportunities to compliment or build up your mate.

Ann lived as though she were a living fortress to shield her beloved Randy. His public office made him vulnerable to criticism. Humor was her forte, and she used it as his fortress, turning intended verbal lances into laughs. Her wit was seasoned with wisdom. She never served as a pipeline for unnecessary negatives aimed at him. Often things injurious to him were kept in the casket of her memory. Lovingly, she sought to reassure him by passing on all comments that might be encouraging.

This resulted in his developing a warm, responsive attitude toward her. By association, he identified her with the reassuring, constructive things she shared. Words and their bearer are often associated.

Look for little things that deserve praise. Botanists who know when and where to look find some of nature's greatest beauty obscured and overshadowed. The rare and delicate beauty of a tiny spring flower might be overlooked by a less sensitive eye. Marriage has a proliferation of these tiny blossoms. Look for them. Make bouquets of them. Praise for the little daily things builds relationships. Expression of appreciation is an indirect form of romance. "You look good in that." "I like the way you handled that." "Thanks for what you did" and similar expressions are all ways of saying "I love you."

While being personally positive, also be sensitive to life's shower of negatives. Be an umbrella. Shield your mate from any negatives you can.

Mark Twain said it takes two persons to injure you: an enemy to malign you and a friend to let you know what the person said. Don't pass on negatives unless they can be used positively.

Envision your role as two-fold regarding building up your mate. One, be a shield against incoming hurtful missiles. Two, be a force that strengthens. The latter may imply that you have the capacity to see weaknesses in your partner. If so, interpret that as a gift of God. God may have given you that capacity not in order that you might criticize, but in order that you might pray for the weakness and work to eliminate it.

In his book entitled *Hide or Seek*, Dr. James Dobson observed that "personal worth is not something human beings are free to take or leave. We must have it and when it is unattainable, everybody suffers."

The person without self-esteem suffers, and so do all associated with him. A devalued person depreciates the worth of a family unit. Lifting your mate's self-esteem affords you a lift, too.

Supernatural strength can be gained by prayer. Praising each other enables a couple to come together at the apex of God's throne. It works in three ways. It prompts the person praying to be more compassionate and considerate. It enlists the Lord in working in the matter. Thus, divine help is gained. Third, both of these combine as a blessing in the life of the one for whom the prayer is offered.

Including the Lord in your plans and problems, rather than

bringing him in belatedly, will enlist heaven itself on the side of your marriage. Ask His help in formulating your plans. Make sure He concurs before you ask Him to bless something of which He might disapprove. This shows both sincerity and respect for His will.

Fellowship Couples must share in all of life. Be open and clear in sharing conversationally. Go places together, do things together, relate to each other.

Some people try to isolate themselves on a protective island, figuring that if they never open themselves, they'll never feel pain. That is a poor philosophy regarding relationships and speaks of a miserable self-image. Such people will someday find themselves on an emotionless desert island. Feelings are a fact; don't try to ignore them. Use them to advantage—the advantage of your marriage.

Marriage is a bond, not bondage. Envision it as something between you that attracts, not something around you that restricts. Friendship becomes a new bonding agent.

After introducing herself to me, a gracious wife said of her husband, "This is my partner." *Partner*—what a beautiful term for one's spouse. There are times this partnership gives strength to the bond. A reliance on each other allows for a demonstration of devotion.

Such a loving partnership has friendship as its basis. Friendship even transcends romance, enhancing it. Lois Wyse speaks of this in her work entitled *Love Poems for the Very Married:*

> Someone asked me
> to name the time
> our friendship stopped
> and love began.
> Oh! my darling
> that's the secret,
> Our friendship
> never stopped.

Sex can be the most intimate form of expression and fellowship. Yet, while its deep emotions can cement a relationship, sex itself cannot solve all problems. Too many have bought the tabloid image of sex, believing sex equals love. It doesn't take long for purely sexual love to become boring and for the persons involved to become bitter, disillusioned, and feeling betrayed. They may start by blaming their partners, but ultimately they end up blaming themselves.

You are to " . . . glorify God in your body . . ." (1 Corinthians 6:20). Why? "For everything created by God is good, and nothing is to be rejected if it is received with thanksgiving" (1 Timothy 4:4 RSV).

The world's mentality depicts love as growing out of sex. The biblical view depicts sex as growing out of love. Sex is a constructive facet of love. It is only one facet, however. There must be a balance. To expect sex to compensate for friendship, compassion, communication, loyalty, devotion, and grace is to end up frustrated and eventually totally disillusioned. Then even sex becomes a burden and disappointment.

To fellowship basically means to do things together. These things need not be expensive or exotic. Try a few of these simple steps to variety.

Exercise together. It's wise to stay in good physical condition at all times. An exercise program should not be allowed to divide you. Companionship, not competition, should result.

Take a walk together. Emphasize the *together* aspect. Gladys and Paul were incessant quibblers and quarrelers. Late in life they learned that walking together brought them together. Changing vistas renew vitality and widen one's vision. Their cue to cool it was "Let's go for a walk."

I have never known of two people who were able to walk and argue at the same time. It is amazing how many times the Bible speaks of people walking together. The result—friendship.

Take your mate on a date. Inexpensive outings can help

keep the marriage from becoming stale. Picnics, with or without ants, are not costly and are always a delight. By refusing to become sedentary, by adventuring together, you can push back new frontiers and explore new horizons all your life.

Toast your little *triumphs* together. Look for little things to celebrate. Don't pass an opportunity to recognize even the most minimal achievement. Salute success of all sizes.

There should be a regular time when you give each other your undivided attention. Schedule times together. Success in other matters should never be allowed to rob you of success in your marriage.

Share regularly in a devotional time together. Take time for it, make time for it. Read a passage of Scripture out loud and pray together daily. This togetherness on a spiritual plane admirably influences every other aspect of life.

Forum The Roman forum was a place of discussion. A primary purpose of the forum was to resolve differences. It was a time to reach an understanding.

"No one can develop freely in this world and find full life," writes Paul Tournier, a noted Christian psychiatrist from Geneva, "without feeling understood by at least one person. Misunderstood, man loses his faith in life or even in God. He is blocked and he regresses."

You are going to have disagreements. Resolve in advance to use them creatively. Determine not to let them divide you but rather to develop you.

Pick a time to talk. Various things influence moods. Be sensitive to each other's mood swing and use it constructively. Never discuss an important matter after 9:30 P.M. Never try to resolve complicated issues immediately before or after a meal.

When disagreements occur, disagree without being disagreeable. Remember, you are discussing an issue, not an individual. Avoid attacking each other's mentality or judgment. Stick to the issue.

Don't wait until there is a crisis to resolve. Talk often, when there are good and positive matters to discuss.

Forgiveness Forgiveness is an essential ingredient in marriage. It must be sought often and given frequently.

Wisely the Bible urges: "be ye kind one to another, tenderhearted, forgiving one another, even as God for Christ's sake hath forgiven you" (Ephesians 4:32).

If the living God, Creator of heaven and earth, can forgive you, one of His lowest creatures, surely you can forgive a peer. Do it out of gratitude for God's forgiveness.

No person deserves God's forgiveness. Perhaps there will be a time when your partner will not deserve your forgiveness and yet will want it. For God's sake, give it. It will also be for the sake of your marriage.

Sooner or later, you are going to need forgiveness. When you get it, show gratitude. This will motivate you to avoid needing further forgiveness for that same error. A grateful response shows appreciation.

Learn to say "I forgive. . . ." There will be many occasions when you will need to say "Please forgive me. . . ."

No one should reserve the right to resurrect something they professed to have forgiven. Be childlike in this matter. Children are quick to forgive and forget.

Faithfulness Unrivaled and unquestioned loyalty is essential to a thriving marriage. Never allow yourself even an act of fantasized unfaithfulness. To do so cultivates the capacity for such conduct. Avoid books, magazines, TV programs, movies, and humor that suggest unfaithfulness is acceptable.

Never give your mate cause for suspicion. Avoid the appearance of evil. Never tease your mate about such a possibility. Any animal can be promiscuous, but only a sincere, dedicated partner can be consistently faithful. A sense of personal gratification and shared fulfillment results from faithfulness.

Avoid statements and circumstances that would feed jealousy. Never consciously do anything to stimulate jealousy.

Leaving and Cleaving

Work at keeping it out of your family life by avoiding things that might cause it. To tease and hint in order to activate jealousy is a cruel torture unbecoming of love. It may be considered coy or cute by the perpetrator, but it is brutal treatment of one you profess to love.

One way to minimize jealousy is to avoid making comparisons. No person likes to be judged. The ego flights and depression resulting from comparisons are improper and unnecessary.

In today's society faithfulness must be a mind set. It requires advance decisions. The advance decision should be, "I will never, under any circumstances, be unfaithful to my marriage vows. I will be loyal to my better self at all times."

Chris Kraft, former head of our nation's manned space program, was once asked, "When is the best time to make a decision?" He responded by noting that the best time to make a decision is before you have to. He went on to explain that before every launch all possible conditions and alternatives are considered. In this manner, no matter what happens in a mission, a decision does not have to be made. The decision was made in calm circumstances, when logic prevailed. In the heat of the moment, they simply have to carry out the decision.

Inevitably, opportunities for unfaithfulness arise in every marriage. The decision to be faithful or unfaithful is always made in advance. The unfaithful person has just waited for what is considered the appropriate moment.

Fight In order to cleave together, a couple must learn to fight. They must know how to fight clean. They must resolve that they will fight *for* their marriage—resolve to fight to keep it alive and growing. Fight against all threats to your union. Confront all adversaries as a twosome. Thus even obstacles and adversities become blessings. They give occasions for team play by two who always play doubles. When two unite in spirit and effort against a common foe, they become better bonded. It furthers the cause of their marriage.

The Bible says, "They twain shall be one." A startled

young bride asked, "*Which* one?" Neither! A new one emerges. Both make a contribution, neither losing personal identity in the new relationship. However, they are absorbed in a cause larger than self. *Me* is no longer the primary consideration. *Us* becomes the issue—*us* against all odds. "I think" and "you think" give way to "we think."

Centuries ago Saint Exupery declared, "Love does not consist in gazing at each other but in looking outward together in the same direction." The home should be the base that serves as the observation point.

My elderly grandparents were a model of cleaving. In their twilight years they often sat together on the porch, not just looking over the farm, but over life. These long, quiet sessions were only occasionally punctuated with an enjoyable interchange. Emotional fires had faded. There were few fresh, new, creative adventures to share. They were nevertheless closer and more in love than ever. They lived out their "till death do us part" commitment happily. Little wonder that when death broke their bond, one soon followed the other to spend eternity together.

Such a mind set enables a couple to realize they are not *stuck* with each other, but they can *stick* with each other.

2

The Plan for Man and Woman

It is said that

"God created the heavens and the earth
and He rested."
Then God created man,
"and He rested."
Next He made woman, and
since that time neither
God nor man
has rested.

Every man should get on his knees and thank God repetitiously for such a beautiful and constructive disruption of his rest.

Adam's longest day was his first—there was no Eve. Without the right relationship with the right person, every day lacks something.

Christ's statement related to the Christian Church has a germane application to the husband-and-wife relationship. It is His intent " . . . that they may be made perfect in one . . . " (John 17:23).

One of life's stellar adventures is observed as "they two became one." To understand that ultimate objective, it is expedient to understand its origins. It is easier to know who we are and where we are going if we know from whence we came.

In the Beginning

Genesis means "beginning." There is a striking passage in the book of beginnings that gives insight into persons' point of origin. (Note: persons is plural, and point is singular.) Having begun together, we are to live peaceably and happily together as husband and wife.

Genesis 2:18–24 contains the historical account of the creation of man and woman. Though this is an actual record of the physical *how* of man's beginning, it contains even more. It also relates to *why* God created male and female.

> And the Lord God said, It is not good that the man should be alone; I will make him an help meet for him. And out of the ground the Lord God formed every beast of the field, and every fowl of the air; and brought them unto Adam to see what he would call them: and whatsoever Adam called every living creature, that was the name thereof. And Adam gave names to all cattle, and to the fowl of the air, and to every beast of the field; but for Adam there was not found an help meet for him. And the Lord God caused a deep sleep to fall upon Adam, and he slept: and he took one of his ribs, and

The Plan for Man and Woman

closed up the flesh instead thereof; And the rib, which the Lord God had taken from man, made he a woman, and brought her unto the man. And Adam said, This is now bone of my bones, and flesh of my flesh: she shall be called Woman, because she was taken out of Man. Therefore shall a man leave his father and his mother, and shall cleave unto his wife: and they shall be one flesh.

Genesis 2:18–24

Verse 18 depicts woman's emergence as subsequent to man's in the sequence. Inquiry is made as to why woman was not created first. The humorous response is, "God did not want any advice on how to make man." The very word *woman* suggests the real reason. *Woman* means to answer. Man is the question; woman is the answer.

A point needs to be established immediately. The order of their origin is not intended to imply superiority or inferiority. They are co-equal, though distinctly diverse.

She was made "an help meet for him." A transliteration of this passage would render it, "I will create for him one who shall tally and correspond with him as a counterpart." Oneness in diversity is intended. Two are to become an intellectual, spiritual, emotional, and physical adaptation of each other. They tally and correspond as counterparts.

The ancient Hebrew in which this was first penned denotes a helper similar to him, as his mirror image. Woman is to be one in which the husband sees his image reflected, or his counterpart. This gives man a great responsibility. He must be certain that he is always projecting the best image. On occasion he may resent his wife and unwittingly be detesting his own reflected image. The answer—her response—may be to an improper action, attitude, or utterance on behalf of the initiator, the husband.

Action-reaction A weighty responsibility is placed on the husband by this concept. Actually, it is a beautiful opportunity and a blessed privilege.

The action-reaction concept contained herein reveals the

action is to be initiated by the husband. The reaction is the response of the wife. Husbands thus have a major role to play in setting the mood and establishing the prevailing atmosphere in the home. This is his responsibility. He is the mood setter, the one who inaugurates attitudes and initiates actions. He must assume the place of loving aggressor in the home. Anything less represents a forfeiture of rights and responsibility. Abuse of this responsibility by excess is repression, and may result in rebellion and resentment.

A *helpmate, not just a mate* In verses 19 and 20 of Genesis 2, Adam is shown observing the natural order around him. He found no counterpart to himself capable of intellectual, emotional, spiritual, and physical response.

God made a mate for all the animals in His creation. But not for man. To have done so would have confirmed certain current concepts stating that the male-female association is basically biological. The sexual involvement of *Homo sapiens* is more than a mere biological urge. It is an involvement of intellectually, emotionally, and spiritually committed responsible persons.

God made woman as a helping being in whom man could recognize himself. Man stood in need of this helper if he was to fulfill the divine decree of Genesis 1:26, 27. In order for man to fulfill his calling, to perpetuate and multiply his race, as well as to cultivate and govern the earth, woman was essential.

> God created the heaven and the earth and He said,
> "It is good."
> He created the night and the day and He said,
> "It is good."
> He created the dry land and the sea and He said,
> "It is good."
> He created the animals and vegetation and He said,
> "It is good."
> God created man and He said,
> "It is *not* good . . .
> that man should be alone."

The Plan for Man and Woman

In that instant man, a mere potential, became an antithesis. These opposites attract and enact in order to become one completed entity.

A rib with a reason *God caused a deep sleep to fall upon Adam.*

This is amplified by Job 33: 15,16: "In a dream, in a vision of the night, when deep sleep falleth upon men, in slumberings upon the bed; Then he openeth the ears of men, and sealeth their instruction."

Man's comprehension and commission regarding life and love began after that nap. This is the golden hour of divine instruction.

And he took one of his ribs. The word rendered *rib* actually means side, or flank. This identifies the portion of the anatomy from which woman was made.

From the rib of man God *built* the female, through whom the human race is to be *built* up in concert with the male. This building up involves much more than mere natural procreation or physical birth. It relates to all facets of life.

An analogy paralleling this physical creation relates to the word *side*, or *ribs*. The *side* is analogous to one of the facets of man's essence. Man is depicted as a many-sided being. Woman is a total development of one of his personality parts. Man has many sides to his nature, but without woman he is incomplete, and vice versa. One plus one equals one. Man and woman are two poles of humanity's sphere, opposite and complementary. Like the stars, they differ in their glory (*see* 1 Corinthians 15:41). Man's basic excellence is virtue. Woman's basic excellence is grace. That is not to imply that one does not have the other. Actually, each enhances the other. It is just that the elementary elements are different.

A perpetual healing *And closed up the flesh instead thereof.*

In addition to referring to man's physical healing, this indicates there is no noticeable outward manifestation of the incompleteness of man. It is man's very *essence*—his nature—that is incomplete without woman. Each completes and complements the total being of the other. The gap is closed by two parts.

The woman was created not from dust of the earth, but from Adam's rib. She was created this way to provide inseparable unity and fellowship of life with man. The mode of her creation established the moral order for marriage. Woman's interdependence with man was established by the order of creation. This forms the root of that tender love with which man is to love the woman as his own body (*see* Ephesians 5:28).

Creation's completion   *Made he a woman.*
Woman is the completion of God's creation—the zenith of His handiwork. With her emergence, creation ceased and cultivation began. Her presence was an enhancement to all that was created before her.

And brought her unto the man. Woman was brought to man in order to relieve his solitude with emotional, spiritual, intellectual, and physical companionship. She cultivates his moral sympathies, inspires his worship of God, increases his intellectual capacity, and excites his admiration and appreciation.

Man must reciprocate by encouraging woman in all of these areas. He must be the aggressor on all four fronts in an endeavor to incite excellence in each area. Any achievement by the woman in any of these domains should garner his accolades.

The two must not be competitors, but completers of each other. The male is the initiator, the female the stimulator. A husband who is an aggressor will find his wife to be the progressor. They are like the two sides of a seesaw; they must be balanced, if the relationship is to function properly.

A second self   *Bone of my bones, and flesh of my flesh.*
The panorama of emerging woman is contained in these couplets. This Hebrew figure of speech meant "she is self of myself." *Bone* in several Semitic dialects was used for "self." She was immediately recognized, without any divine revela-

tion, as man's second self (technically, "my very own self"). Woman is man's essential peer, his *alter ego*.

This adds additional credibility to loving one's wife as one's own self, since they are as concentric layers in the same sphere. Few men would consider ignoring, insulting, injuring, criticizing, cursing, abusing, or misusing themselves, and there is something missing in the life of the man who does any of these to his wife. Such conduct is a symptom of an inner sickness.

Flesh of my flesh represents woman as man's counterpart of feeling and sensing. In this her best reflective facet is revealed. She is an embodiment of those tender and gentle qualities of life. This is a side that man does not so easily show.

She shall be called Woman. She is called woman (in the Hebrew, *isha*) because she came from man (*ish*). She is formed out of his solidity (bone) and sensibility (flesh), therefore her title—woman. In English, the qualification *wo* before *man* merely indicates a difference of sex. In Latin, she is called the *mulier,* a word derived from *mollior,* meaning softer and more tender.

This ancient account is the basis for a wife assuming the name of her husband; it shows her identification with and response to the man.

Why Man First?

Why did God make man first, instead of woman? In jest, it has been suggested that He practiced on man what He perfected in woman. There is a biblical reason, however. Man was made in the image of God. If both man and woman had been created simultaneously, an essential feature of divine likeness would have been forfeited. As the Absolute One, there is no duality in God. Monotheism is indicative of Him.

The unity of the pair is established by the primary creation of one individual from whom the other was derived. Unity in diversity is evidenced by one emerging from the other.

Three important events occurred in the life of Adam before the creation of Eve. First, he was installed in the garden as owner, keeper, and dresser. Secondly, as their rational superior, he reviewed the animals. Thirdly, in an interview with his Maker he came to understand language, and during his inspection and naming of the animals, he first employed it. Since susceptive and conceptive powers of understanding are inherent to speech, Adam was qualified to hold rational conversations with beings like himself.

By the first event, Adam was prepared to provide for the sustenance and comfort of his wife. By the second, he became aware of his power to protect her. By the third, he had an established relationship with God and had developed the capacity for fellowship with woman. Having met with his superior (God) and his inferiors (the animals), he was now ready to meet with his equal.

Man's responsibility Those same factors are areas of man's responsibility toward woman today. He is to:

Provide for her sustenance and comfort. The man should provide her with food, clothing, and shelter (*see* Genesis 3:19). The man who fails to do so because of dereliction is worse than an infidel (*see* 1 Timothy 5:8).

Protect her physically and psychologically. Woman is physically weaker and deserving of protection (*see* 1 Peter 3:7). Psychologically he should boost her and lift her emotionally (*see* Proverbs 31:28).

Permeate life with a spiritual and moral tone. He should afford informed and inspiring initiative in spiritual matters (*see* 1 Timothy 2:4). A genuine foundation of fundamental faith should be established and expanded (*see* 2 Timothy 3:16,17).

Woman needs and wants these three aspects of life cared for by her husband. Scripturally these are represented as instinctive. The society that plays these down rebels against God's order. The woman who protests them violates God's will. The man who forfeits them transgresses God's design.

Had Adam and Eve both sprung from the earth, they might have related to each other as brother and sister. However, the love for which they were designed was not of this type. Adam's love for Eve was to be that of "a friend that sticketh closer than a brother." The great purpose of God's order for their creation was marriage. For this reason, the avowed obligations of marriage are considered sacred. No experimentation is needed to see if marriage will work; it was *designed* to work, if its God-given order is followed. As the ring symbolizes love, so it is to be enduring and unending.

Happiness Is

Comparing Adam and Eve's relationship to that of Jesus and the Church shows the strategic significance of marriage. "Husbands," said Paul, "love your wives, even as Christ also loved the church, and gave himself for it" (Ephesians 5:25).

The marriage of Adam and Eve, and the institution of marriage in general, is symbolic of Christ and His Church. This reveals the deep and abiding mystery of the marriage relationship. "Husbands, love your wives..."

Keep on loving your second self—as yourself. She will respond in refreshing and rewarding love. You can be the husband of a happy wife, which is the way God designed marriage to work. To be happy, take the initiative in making *her* happy. Happiness is not a goal to be sought or an object to be bought; happiness is a beautiful by-product of a job well done. To attain it, conduct a campaign to make your wife happy. The more successful you are in doing that, the happier you will be.

3

How to Be a Winning Wife

For an arrow to reach its mark, the bow must yield to the string. As the string draws the bow, the bow must respond with its strength. Neither the bow nor the string alone can speed an arrow to its mark. One must draw, the other must yield; together they have power.

Likewise, two persons can ride the same horse. Of necessity, one must sit in front of the other. Neither is superior; neither is inferior. They simply have different positions and roles. Each may well complement the function of the other, and thus both will be fulfilled.

In any organization, there must be order and system. The role and function of each person in the structure must be defined, since better definition results in better relationships.

In marriage there are also different functions and roles to be fulfilled. All are of equal importance. To argue which is more important, the husband or the wife, is as futile as arguing which blade of a pair of scissors is more important, or which sleeve of a shirt is superior. Without the other, either is dramatically lacking—each is essential to the other.

To dispute whether the right or left shoe is more important is absurd. Each one fulfilling its function is equal in importance to the other. However, if one shoe exchanges places with the other, neither can fulfill its role. The issue isn't importance, but individuality.

Comedies have been written about husbands and wives exchanging roles. In real life, it is a tragedy, not a comedy.

After seven years in the role of house-husband and child caretaker, Jim sobbed his heart out to me. He told me he had been robbed of his sense of masculinity and his identification as a husband and father. He had become sexually impotent, anxious, and insecure. Gail, his wife, was an attorney with a dominant personality. In being the breadwinner, she had made the same mistake many males make, and had forced Jim into dependency. Finally his feelings surfaced and an explosion was averted only through extensive counseling and a balancing of their roles and relationships.

Tami was a pediatrician. John, her husband, had a respectable job with a modest income. He had great pride in her, and she had great esteem for him. They understood and accepted each other's accomplishments, supporting each other with admiration and enthusiasm. Neither felt threatened. In their marriage they assumed the biblical roles and each fulfilled the prescribed function. Both were even more gratified by their ability to accept each other and live a fulfilled life.

God, who designed our roles, has defined our functions. He made us compatible, he created us to complete and complement each other. There is excitement in the two becoming one.

Peter was an instrument of the Lord, communicating to us

insights regarding the roles of husbands and wives. The truths that follow are extracted from 1 Peter 3:1–7.

> Likewise, ye wives, be in subjection to your own husbands; that, if any obey not the word, they also may without the word be won by the conversation of the wives; While they behold your chaste conversation coupled with fear. Whose adorning let it not be that outward adorning of plaiting the hair, and of wearing of gold, or of putting on of apparel; But let it be the hidden man of the heart, in that which is not corruptible, even the ornament of a meek and quiet spirit, which is in the sight of God of great price. For after this manner in the old time the holy women also, who trusted in God, adorned themselves, being in subjection unto their own husbands: Even as Sara obeyed Abraham, calling him lord: whose daughters ye are, as long as ye do well, and are not afraid with any amazement. Likewise, ye husbands, dwell with them according to knowledge, giving honour unto the wife, as unto the weaker vessel, and as being heirs together of the grace of life; that your prayers be not hindered.
>
> 1 Peter 3:1–7

It should be noted that this passage deals with the relationship between husbands and wives, *not* men and women. This is critical to understanding what follows. Those who try to apply this passage to men and women in general not only misinterpret the passage but also miss the intended spirit.

Peter first addressed the wife. The Greek work is *gune*, which appears 220 times in the New Testament. You can hear in the word our root for "gynecology."

Peter noted six commendable characteristics of a winning wife.

Submission

The wife is urged to be in subjection. It is expedient to note again that this is an exhortation for wives to be in subjection to their own husbands. It does not imply that any woman is to be subjected to all men just because of her femininity. The force of the statement as regards husbands and wives is made clear by the statement being an imperative that involves continuing conduct.

This does not hint at inferiority of sex, person, character, or role. Superiority and inferiority are not the issue—order is.

Submission deals with one whose role ranks under another's role. This principle is observable in all of life. The role of an all-American running back ranks under that of his quarterback. Their roles are different, but either without the other is incomplete. The first violinist fulfills a vital role that is subordinate to the conductor, but each complements the other. Teamwork requires each person to fulfill his assigned role. Each is a part of the other and involved with all others.

First Peter 3:1 is encouragement to relate and to respond willingly to one whose *role* you respect. This respect is primarily for the position and secondarily for the person. It does not hint of any inferiority of roles. It is intended to establish the structure, function, and order in a household, and it should not be overlooked that it does speak clearly of subordination in *function* within the intimate sphere of the home.

Every body must have a head to function; every institution must have a head for practical purposes.

Any husband who is trying to force his wife into such a role is engaged in a futile effort. Husbands who try to live as overlords are violating the spirit of this principle. The wife's role is not one of spineless submission or cringing cowardice. Ideally hers is a submission of perfect love, not fear. It is voluntary selflessness. Any attentive, loving husband should respectfully and responsibly relate to such a winning wife.

Fortunate is the wife whose husband is a God-fearing, wife-loving man. Not all wives are so fortunate. The text takes this into account and promises hope to a wife who lives by the standard of God's Word in the presence of an ungodly husband.

Even if she is married to a man who does not obey the

Word of God, she might win him to faith in Christ through her obedience to God's Word in submitting to him as her husband. In speaking of such a husband, the expression "obey not" is used. It identifies one in a state of obstinate rejection of the Gospel. Such a husband can never be brought to God by a wife who is disobedient to God's Word.

For nineteen years Lee lived with a brutish, brooding husband. Sure, there were good times, but the prevalent bad times cast a shadow over their relationship. He was as indifferent to her faith as he was insensitive to her needs. Her virtues went unacclaimed, while her occasional shortcomings were accented. Privately he ignored her good points, and publicly he criticized her weak ones. In his mind he was the lord, she the servant. That philosophy made much of life miserable for Lee.

Uncompromisingly and uncomplainingly, she lived her faith before him. Those who observed their relationship marveled that she never retaliated in kind. Her grace contrasted with his gruffness.

In light of his inflexibility, many urged her to leave him. They had taken note of his obnoxious behavior while overlooking one factor in Lee's life: She loved Bob. She was not ignorant of or unaffected by his master-servant concept of marriage.

Her love for the Lord and His Word prompted her to ignore advice to leave Bob. She knew from Scripture what her role was and how she should relate to Bob. She lived with an abiding confidence that, just as there are principles in physics that produce predictable results, so there are guidelines in marriage that yield foreseeable consequences. Her love for Bob and her faith in biblically prescribed principles enabled her to be consistent in her life.

As a tiny candle warms a mass by consistently glowing, she was ever so imperceptibly melting Bob's cool heart and warming his spirit. Though he would not read the Bible and resented her reading it, he was residing with a living Bible—Lee. It wasn't what someone taught that changed his life, it was what he caught from his now-beloved Lee. It created in him a desire to be as much of a role model of the biblically defined husband as she had been of a wife.

What if Lee had not known of this promise in the Scripture? The happy life shared by these two after both accepted their rightful role in the relationship could never have been enjoyed without consistency. Said Lee, "I would gladly do it all over again for the joy gained with the man I love."

Not Nagging

The word translated *conversation* in 1 Peter 3:1 does not refer to speech alone, but actually means "life-style" in general. However, here it does relate to conversation.

Nagging never draws a person to our position or our person. One husband said, "Every time anything goes wrong, my wife becomes historical."

A friend replied, "You mean hysterical?"

"No," was the reply, "I mean historical. She brings up everything in my past that I have done wrong."

Solomon, a man who should know, said, "A nagging wife is like water dripping endlessly" (Proverbs 19:13 NEB). Anyone who has tried to rest or sleep where there is dripping water can understand just how irritating nagging can be.

Again the sage Solomon noted, "Better to live in a corner of a house-top than have a nagging wife and a brawling household" (Proverbs 21:9 NEB).

Charles Spurgeon observed, "God save us all from wives who are angels in the streets, saints in the church, and devils at home." Consistency is a virtue.

To avoid nagging, pick your moment and mood lovingly and make your statement clearly. Make it understood, so it doesn't have to be restated. If a point is understood and not responded to, repetition isn't likely to do anything but irritate. Undue repetition is not likely to achieve more than a positive initial statement.

To determine the value of nagging, stop and reflect on how you personally respond to anyone nagging you. Do you respond positively? Do you have a tendency to react, rather than act? In this regard, others are no different from you.

Chastity

Again the word *conversation* appears in the writing of Peter (1 Peter 3:2). Here it refers to one's total life-style. It is preceded by the word *chaste*. This translates the Greek *hagnen*, which literally means "pure." The text is an appeal to be the epitome of moral purity.

Today's language is laden with moral booby traps. It is, however, no more or less so than in the biblical era. For that reason, wives are urged to be chaste. The word was used to describe metals without alloys that weaken. Thus the appeal to avoid contaminants.

Contaminants are most often cleverly camouflaged. Popularized glamour is a deceptive device. Sue, a sweet, devoted young wife, showed disdain at first when her new friends spoke of the excitement of daytime soap operas on television. The popularity of such programming caused the idea of viewing to become beguiling. Nominal initial interest inspired by intrigue soon turned Sue into a soap-opera junkie. Within a year, her entire day's routine was built around her favorites.

Almost imperceptively at first, certain speech patterns were adopted from her new heroines. Gradually their gestures became hers. Others noticed her unconscious evolution into a personality that her previous self would not have recognized and would have abhorred. Sweet Sue became seductive Sue. It happened mentally long before reality ruptured her formerly happy marriage. Seductiveness had subtly become the alloy that weakened her total life-style. An idea became an ideal that resulted in an immoral involvement.

Centuries ago, a pertinent question was asked by Ezekiel: "How should we then live?" (*see* Ezekiel 33:10.)

Be alert. Jesus' warning to Simon is applicable to us, for Satan wants to "sift you as wheat" (*see* Luke 22:31). To *sift* means to separate. There are tempting things in life that tear us apart inside and divide married couples. Be mindful that there are things devised and designed to divide. Avoid them. Don't flirt with them. One of the best ways to avoid yielding to temptation is to stay away from it.

Avoidance of contaminants is essential. If pure water is desired, don't put it where pollutants can get in it. If you desire pure conduct, don't expose yourself to moral pollutants. Avoid novels, magazines, and TV programs with suggestive themes. Don't compromise with yourself; establish your standards and don't lower them. Many who drop their ideals do it without realizing—they simply jump from the concept to the conclusion without proper consideration. Correct consideration may well reveal the conclusion to be corrupting in character.

Monitoring the mind makes Christian thoughts possible and helps us prevent thoughts we do not want reflected in our conduct. If an impure thought occurs, recycle the subject. That is, don't leave the subject simply by dismissing the thought. Before forgetting the idea, rethink the topic from a chaste viewpoint. Leave the topic with a positive, pure conclusion. "Let this mind be in you, which was also in Christ Jesus" (Philippians 2:5). Think the Christ-thought. Steps to prevention are much easier than those to repentance.

Resolve to be a living answer to the aged question: "Who can find a virtuous woman?" Be alert; that resolve will be tested!

Playing with an immoral thought is like playing with a ball filled with air in a swimming pool. No matter how many times or how deep you push it under the the water, it will surface again. An unchaste idea filed in your mental bank will surface again and again. Deflate the ball and keep it out of the pool.

Paul exhorted young Timothy to flee youthful lusts (2 Timothy 2:22). The term means to run so fast you kick up dust. A worthy postscript: "Don't leave a forwarding address."

Benjamin Needler, a writer of Puritan vintage, observed,

"We must not part with sin, as with a friend, with the purpose to see it again and to have the same familiarity with it as before, or possibly greater.... We must shake our hands of it as Paul did the viper off his hand into the fire."

Affection

People want to express their feelings, which only becomes wrong when they are expressed to the wrong person or in improper places.

In marriage, expressions of affection should involve all three types of love noted by the Greek words for love: *Eros*, which is sexual in nature; *philia*, which is friendship, a brotherly love; and *agape*, a self-giving love. Christ's love for you is a model of *agape* love. The last two types serve to enrich sexual love. *Agape* elevates *eros* from self-gratification to caring concern for the other's welfare. *Philia* fulfills *eros*, making it personal and considerate. *Eros* alone is never fulfilling. Fascination with sexual love, without *philia* and *agape* love, is the great American deception—it is an unfulfilled promise.

Affection involves expressions of love—expressions through both action and inaction. Much has been said about doing little delightful things to show affection. It is good to give a gift when no occasion calls for it, to send a card when not required, to publicly compliment, and to leave an unexpected love note. However, it is just as essential to avoid little irritating acts or expressions.

When a certain thing is known to irritate your partner, don't do it. Regardless of how enjoyable it might be to you to chew ice, don't do it if your mate is irritated by it. By cutting out agitating actions, love and affection are indirectly shown.

Learn the likes and dislikes of your partner and use this knowledge for your mutual advantage. Sensitivity to the traits your mate likes in you will enable you to develop them. You can consciously cultivate your virtues and curb your vices, a study that should be a lifelong undertaking. Look for ways to grow together.

Modesty

Peter advises, "Whose adorning let it not be that outward adorning . . . " (1 Peter 3:3). This is an appeal to strive for beauty not found in mere outward appearances. It is an exhortation to avoid excessive adornment.

The Greek word translated as adorning is *kosmos*, which means orderliness. When extremes in apparel are practiced, the result is chaos—a word that is a mirror of some styles now in vogue. Some women wear so much eye shadow that they look like a jack-o'-lantern with a blown out candle. Others use hairstyles resembling shredded wheat. Some coiffures look like they were designed by Roto-Rooter. Such efforts in apparel and appearance are intended to attract attention to themselves. A person who must depend on such gimmicks is likely lacking in a wholesomely appealing character.

Not only does the Bible encourage people to base their appeal on character rather than outward appearance, studies now reveal this is what more people are looking for in a mate. A large segment of college students were asked to list the qualities they look for in a potential date. Looks ranked near the bottom of the list. Such things as personality, sincerity, and character took precedence over physical appearance.

At Oregon State University an unidentified student attended a speech class in a big black bag, with only his feet visible. The teacher, who knew the bag's occupant, observed the various responses of the other students. The class mood swung from hostility to curiosity and finally to friendliness. The class actually became fond of "bag man." Why? The bag was not exceptionally attractive—actually, it was without appeal—but the student's personality, sincerity, and character were evident, even through a bag.

In certain countries veils are lifted only after marriage. The couple gets to know each other's character before becoming absorbed with countenance. When a marriage is based principally on physical features, its future isn't good. Beauty has a natural tendency to atrophy; character, however, can be enhanced with each passing year.

A good relationship must be based on a Godlike view of your partner. Samuel said, " . . . man looketh on the outward appearance, but the Lord looketh on the heart" (1 Samuel 16:7).

What virtues of the heart are worth developing? Modesty itself is a trait of the heart. One's external appearance is only a reflection of the mind. Some people are considered sexy because they dress sexy, but the truth is they *think* sexy, and thus dress the role. Grace, charm, dignity, and modesty are mental attitudes that are also detectable from one's outward appearance.

Modesty is a trait that evidences self-confidence apart from being self-centered. A modest person is confident of having a right spirit and proper attitude, so there is no need to strive to attract undeserved attention through a wardrobe designed by jungle tribesmen.

Never fail to show taste in attire and grooming. Use it as an enhancement, never as a deception.

Respect

Peter used an idiom for respect: "coupled with fear" (*see* 1 Peter 3:2). This fear has nothing to do with terror or anxiety; it is merely an appeal for respect. Mutual respect is vital to a relationship. If there is no respect, there is no trust or confidence, and worth is diminished.

Avoid those things that erode respect. Be courteous, not rude. Exercise manners and avoid the crass. Show regard for the other's opinions. Maintain those little grace traits that were so effective during courtship. Never belittle another's opinion in public. If necessary, wait for a private moment and explain your opinion.

Respect is based on trust. Joseph refused to enforce the law against Mary and have her "put away." He respected her to the point that he believed the unbelievable when she told it to him. That took trust. One earns trust by being trustworthy. In marriage it is essential that each partner work at developing the other's trust.

If a person has respect for the vow of marriage, he will strive to remain trustworthy. With our mobile society, it is easy to avoid detection in doing evil. If a person does not have proper respect for the marriage vow, it is simple to violate it. A partner in marriage should resolve to maintain a respectable image.

Unfortunately, there are partners in marriage who violate trust and do not deserve respect. It is at this point that once again the person and the position must be separated in our thinking. The *person* may not be deserving of respect—the *office* of husband or wife is always deserving. Therefore, if you can't respect the person, do show regard for the position. This can sustain you until the person realizes the necessity of restoring respect.

When a person knows respect is being shown, it motivates a desire to be even more respectable. An action-reaction condition develops, where the more respect is given, the more one desires to deserve it. Conversely, the less respect given, the less the desire to earn it.

Sarah used a title of respect for Abraham—the Hebrew word *lord*, which was a title of respect and dignity. Her respect in turn earned her his respect.

Inward Beauty

Peter's sixth facet of a winning wife is inward beauty. He referred to it as " ... the hidden man of the heart ... " (1 Peter 3:4).

George Hermes wisely observed, "A beautiful chaste woman is the perfect workmanship of God and the whole wonder of the world."

A French proverb states: "Beauty, unaccompanied by virtue, is a flower without perfume."

Peter further defined inward beauty as a meek and quiet spirit. Those two terms deserve further development.

The word *meek* means controlled. It was the word used to describe the soldiers of the Roman army. This usage shows that being meek does not mean being cowered, suppressed, or domineered. It is a word for order, speaking of having purpose and being constructively constrained.

The same word was used to describe a wild stallion who had been brought in from the desert. When the animal was bridled and reins placed in controlling hands, the animal was referred to as being meek. It was still strong, energetic, and dynamic, but it now had purpose and direction. When a person puts the reins of life in the hands of Jesus Christ, that life is controlled by Him. When this is done, there is purpose and direction in life.

A controlled life does not express itself volatilely. When a Western mind thinks of strength, it thinks of steel. The Oriental mind envisions water. Water waits its moment, conforming to the contour of its container. It may wait for years behind a large earthern dam, the configuration of the lake determining its shape. When there is a tiny hole in the dam, the water gently seeps through. As it does, it opens the hole a bit more. It works slowly at first, but eventually it exerts its force and washes away the dam.

Many obstacles must be removed in marriage, but they can only be removed by a controlled temperament. Remember, it is the *obstacle* to a good marriage that you want removed, not the marriage itself.

For years friends pleaded with Polly to leave Ted. She was frequently reminded that he was a drunken, no-good goof. She knew all of this. She also remembered her vow of commitment. She endured absurd abuse for over twenty years. Neglect and disrespect was a way of life for her. She knew her treatment came from a drug, not from her beloved Ted. Like water in a lake, she waited, controlled. Then, in a moment of crisis, Ted turned to Christ. His new life in Christ transformed him totally. His love for his beloved and abused wife emerged expressively. The years of waiting were worth it. Polly and Ted were one, bonded by a renewed love. If she had not had a controlled temperament, she would have lost her marriage and Ted would never have come to know the Lord.

Peter also identified inward beauty as a quiet spirit. This speaks of self-discipline. This is gentle dynamite. It does the work of a great force without the explosive quality.

Jan loved her Tony. She also loved the Lord. Tony didn't. He loved her, but thought her love for the Lord was a flaw in an otherwise lovable person. She tried unsuccessfully to share her faith for fifteen years. She even tried reading her daily Bible study out loud, hoping to impress him with some of the truth. To keep from hearing it, he would whistle. Thus they both irritated each other. She exercised self-discipline and increased wisdom. By her gently consistent love for him and her Lord, Tony was drawn to Christ. Since that day, their life together has been a duet, not a duel. Their uncommon common faith has given their marriage a new bond and removed the old bondage. The consistency of her self-discipline drew him to his wife and his Lord.

The time required in these two cases is worth noting. It took Polly twenty years and Jan fifteen to reach their husbands. No amount of preaching could have brought about the dynamic change enjoyed in both marriages, for it was not words that won their husbands, but it was the example of a controlled, disciplined wife that made the difference in both cases.

How to be a winning wife? Peter's description is intended to be effective not only in winning a husband's love but of also winning the husband to Christ. In 1 Peter 3:1, Peter spoke of husbands who obey not the word (that is, nonbelievers) being won without the word. It is the life-style of the wife that is used of the Lord to win the husband. Her example—not her expressions—results in becoming a winning wife.

It does matter whether you win or lose, but whether you win or lose depends on how you play the game. These precepts of Peter might not always work. However, it is certain that nothing else will. Accept the challenge of applying the principles; they are your only sure way of being a winning wife.

4

How to Be a Huggable Husband

It was the time of day when almost no one shops for groceries. The store was empty except for one elderly lady who cautiously made her way to one specific check-out line. Though all lines were open, she passed several to get to one special one.

The cashier, unbeknown to her, was a seminary student working to help pay his way through school. They had seen each other for several weeks. She always waited to go through his line. After exchanging brief pleasantries, she looked around to be sure no one was waiting, then said, "I always wait to go through your line. Do you know why?"

His reply was a respectful, "No, ma'am."

Softly she continued, "I am an old lady. My children are grown and live far away with all of my grandchildren. I live alone, and they rarely visit me. The reason I always go through your line is you always touch my hand when you give me change. There are a lot of weeks you are the only person who ever touches me."

A minister told that story one Sunday morning and concluded by urging people to reach out and touch the person nearest them at that moment. "A simple touch means so much," he said.

Joe and Helen were viewing the service on television. They had been separated for nearly a year, and he had dropped by to pick up the last of his things. It was to be their final goodbye; he had come to move out. They were standing close to each other when the minister urged everyone to reach out and touch the nearest person. Joe gently reached out and touched Helen's hand—a touch that changed their relationship. Instead of moving out, Joe moved back in.

How long has it been since you reached out to really touch somebody?

There are many ways to touch: a look, a smile, a word, a note, or a kind deed are all ways of touching without coming in direct contact. There is also the delightful direct way to touch called a hug. Remember when hugging was reflexive, spontaneous, and fun? Is this instinctive impulse still alive in your marriage? If not, it can and should be revived. A good big-league hug is a splendid way of saying, "I love you." Actually it says, "You are lovable." A hug enables a person to identify with and show affection for another. A well-timed hug feels good, physically and emotionally. It feels good to the one being hugged but even better to the hugger. When a person hugs for the sake of hugging and not in order to be hugged, he is exercising the art in its highest form.

Hugging is life's best form of nonverbal communication. It can actually help open broken channels of verbal communication. A deaf-mute knows a hug says love. I have never hugged a person when it did not result in a big, warm smile in return.

Remember when you were huggable? What happened? When hugs go, it is a symptom that something is missing in the marriage. This external expression can become impulsive again.

Simon Peter identified three characteristics that make a person huggable in 1 Peter 3:7: "Likewise, ye husbands, dwell with them according to knowledge, giving honour unto the wife, as unto the weaker vessel, and as being heirs together of the grace of life; that your prayers be not hindered."

First, Peter addressed husbands here. The Anglo-Saxon root word means house band. It implies that a primary role of the husband is to hold the household together. By him the members of the family are to be made as one.

Dramatic evidence exists that indicates a broad based failing by the husbands of our land. The home has become America's most violent place. A Harris poll revealed that 10 percent of the women interviewed had been physically abused by their husbands within the previous twelve months. Less than 3 percent had been assaulted outside the home.

Over 700,000 children are reportedly abused annually. It is estimated that five times that number go unreported. That may in part explain why nearly 2,000,000 children run away from home annually. The dangers that exist for children in the streets of America are well-known. In light of this, one runaway said, "It is better to be beaten by a stranger on the street than by someone you care about at home."

Sociological findings indicate that if the present incidences of child neglect, child abuse, and child molestation continue, we can expect a proliferation of drug abuse, teenage suicide, violent crimes, and sex perversion. The former are the roots, the latter the fruits. The husband and father can be a force that turns this trend around by leading the family to band together.

An unknown source in the mid 1950's noted some humorous challenges to the husband. These husbands are still to be pitied:

How to Be a Huggable Husband

1. The husband who discovers that, though his wife sure can dish it out, she can't cook it.
2. The husband whose wife keeps telling him to pull in his stomach—after he already has.
3. The husband who returned for credit a book entitled *How to Be Master in Your Own Home*, explaining sheepishly, "My wife won't let me keep it."
4. The husband whose wife made him drink thirty cups of coffee a day to cure his dreadful snoring. After six months she boasted, "He never snores at all any more. He just percolates."
5. The husband who was found shaving at the edge of a lake. A policeman asked, "Haven't you got a bathroom?"

"I certainly have," answered the husband gruffly. "I also have a wife and four daughters."

6. The husband whose son, a freshman in college, reported, "I've landed my first part in a varsity show. I play a man who has been married twenty years."

"Good work, son," exclaimed the dad. "Keep it up and the first thing you know, they'll be giving you a speaking part."

7. The husband who brought his boss home for dinner, exclaiming, "You are about to meet the finest little helpmate, the swellest cook, the best little housekeeper a man ever had—that is, of course, if she is at home."

8. The husband who reported this division of his income to the IRS: 40 percent for food, 30 percent for shelter, and 50 percent for his wife's clothing and amusement. "But that makes 120 percent," protested the agent.

"You don't have to tell me," sighed the husband, "I know it."

Even those eight husbands could benefit from applying the factors suggested by the Apostle Peter in 1 Peter 3:7 as being rudimentary to a good relationship.

Husbands are to dwell with their wives ". . . according to

knowledge. . . ." This means husbands are to be considerate. The text specifically means according to *Christian* knowledge.

Christian knowledge advocates speaking the truth in love.

Communication

Communication is a critical part of living together. It involves words, but even more than words. Surveys reveal the average couple converses about sixteen minutes a day. Even then, much communication is superficial. On what level do you communicate?

Symbols and clichés On this level, most communication consists of code words and formula phrases. "Hi" rates high among these. "How are you doing?" is a good one, if you don't bother to listen to the answer. This is the weakest form of communication.

Statistics and reports TV or radio reports, newspaper stories, or what a person said are shared. These are essential communications, yet they tell nothing about your true self. Communication on this level consists of external statements; the principles are shared, but the person is not involved.

Summaries and opinions Unfortunately this is the ultimate depth of communication for most married couples. Brief, terse comments are shared and acknowledged. This is still superficial communication, since there is little discussion involved. It is merely shared statements, not substance.

Sensitivities and feelings When a person feels secure in a relationship, openness results. An awareness that you care enables a person to drop his guard and open up. There is a degree of vulnerability and trust here. People who fear being misjudged will never get to this level. People will only share their feelings with those they are confident will be understanding. Confidences and intimacies in an interacting environment are shared in this form of relationship.

Souls and spirits This is communication at its best. This involves open, truthful sharing of one's inner self. Loving objectivity is required for a person to be willing to be this transparent. People privileged to enjoy this form of communication are fortunate—it is such a joyous relationship that couples should work ambitiously to restore it. It existed in your courtship, and just as it was vital in beginning your relationship, it is now essential to maintaining it.

To help return to this latter form of relating, remember: You can't talk to a person about a subject they don't want to talk about, when they don't want to talk about it. This is an axiom that does not change. Don't waste your energy trying and thus create an even greater breach. When communication is broken by anger, *stop* and allow a cooling-off period. Never allow yourselves the luxury of both getting mad at the same time. In order to behave rationally, keep your temper under control. If it isn't, don't try to communicate.

Avoid being dogmatic. You may be right, but when opinions differ and you're dogmatic, you are building a wall between yourself and others. Ask probing questions. Try to find the logic and reason in your partner's position. If necessary, agree to disagree. Be sure this is done amicably. Never leave a topic in a state of deep freeze. Make sure the relationship is warm, not hot, and by no means frigid.

To help re-establish better communication, try:

1. Listening. Be attentive to words and the feelings they express.
2. Break the cycle of mutual retaliation. Don't feel that it is essential to have the final word on every subject.
3. Acknowledge the need to work together to improve your communications.
4. Resolve to learn from conflict. Thus, even disagreements can become useful.
5. Acknowledge pain and pleasure in your relationship.

This requires openness. You must establish objectives and state means of reaching them.

6. Discover and develop new ways of relating to each other on a pleasant, positive, and productive level.

7. Expand your extended family. The church is the best possible place to develop new friendships that will strengthen your relationships.

Politeness

Politeness is surely according to Christian knowledge. A verse worthy of decorating the walls of your memory is Ephesians 4:32, "And be ye kind one to another, tenderhearted, forgiving one another, even as God for Christ's sake hath forgiven you." Kindness is a cultivatable quality. Never stop showing it simply because there is no favorable response. Do it not in order to get, but because of what you get out of showing it. Aspire to be known as a kind person.

A kind person feels no necessity of domineering another. He respects the other's personality, convictions, and character. Grace words should garnish the speech as parsley does a delicious dish.

Mary Poppins taught a generation that a spoonful of sugar makes the medicine go down. There are sincere "sugar words" that make unpleasant sharing more palatable. Learn them and use them in sincerity.

Show kindness by little things such as opening the door, pulling out a chair, paying a compliment, doing a favor, and always doing more than has to be done. Do the grace deed—not because it has to be done, but because your nature demands that you do it.

Never forget the importance of little courtesies. They are as important after marriage as before. Indeed, they are actually more essential after, since if they stop, they diminish those expressed before marriage, making them look like mere come-ons. Before marriage those bonus acts of kindness were called courting. They should be kept up all through life; need for them never ceases.

A quality for which there is a growing need in marriage is

spoken of as being tenderhearted. This refers to consideration, affection, concern, compassion, and understanding. It involves feeling *with* the other person.

Strange as it seems, crudeness, crassness, rudeness, and abruptness sometimes are considered cute and excusable during courtship. If you got away with it then, don't plan on getting away with it forever. It soon diminishes in value. Such conduct is so base that it debases.

Everyone likes to feel understood, accepted, and approved. A tenderhearted person gives such assurance. Without it, your mate becomes offended and undervalued. A person in such a state is vulnerable to the first flirt that pays a casual compliment. Your mate's appetite for recognition and praise must be fed by you. If you do, your mate will have no taste for a tempting compliment.

Most people in business would lose all their business if they related to their clients as they do their mate. "Thank you," "Excuse me," and "I appreciate that," are not only good for business but also good for home life.

Forgiveness

Forgiveness is vital to freshness. Most of us make so many mistakes that we need frequent opportunities to begin again. A request for forgiveness means "I love you and regret injuring you. I want to start over and do better. Please give me another chance."

It has been said that a good marriage consists of two good forgivers.

All should be forgiving because we all frequently need forgiveness. Remember, the unforgiving are unforgiven because they are unforgivable.

If you find it difficult to forgive, remember who has forgiven you of what. God, your superior, has forgiven you. He didn't do it because you are so forgivable, but because He is so forgiving. If God, your superior, can forgive you, can't you forgive a peer?

If you can't forgive your mate for her sake, do it for Jesus' sake. Show your gratitude to Him for His forgiveness by forgiving someone in His name. This is an indirect way of saying, "Thank You, Lord."

Remember how good you felt as a child when your parents forgave you for something? There was a sense of release. You were drawn toward the one who forgave you. That same trait is still alive in all of us. When you forgive someone, they are drawn toward you, bringing two alienated persons into alliance.

People who cherish feelings of resentment and never learn to forget are harboring an embryo of hate. Even when you are not able to forget the historical nature of the situation, you can forgive and forget the bitterness.

Bitterness does more harm to the vessel in which it is stored than to the one on which it is poured. Forgiveness is the handle by which you flush bitterness out of your life—enjoy forgiving.

Common politeness motivates a person to say, "I forgive." When done, delight in it, as you and the one forgiven will be drawn closer to each other.

Christ commented that the one who loves Him most is the one He has forgiven most. This principle applies in marriage also. If there is much to be forgiven, it can be a bond for your union.

For years my beloved father-in-law had been a car dealer. The era of the import was just beginning. A sleek little import glistened in his showroom when a friend asked for a demonstration ride. Happily they got in. Papa Knight looked over his shoulder and instinctively put the car in what had always been reverse. Still looking back, he accelerated, sure he would go backward. The car moved forward, right through the showroom display window. He didn't know how to put the car in reverse.

Many husbands seem to have no reverse in their personality. They don't know how to back up and say, "I'm sorry." A car without a reverse gear would be diminished in value—a marriage without a reverse gear is a disaster.

Every macho man needs to be reminded that "Pride goeth before destruction, and an haughty spirit before a fall" (Proverbs 16:18). Love enables you to back up with an appropriate apology and start over. It can get you out of lots of tight spots.

When forgiveness is sought and offered, there should be "no record of wrongs" (*see* 1 Corinthians 13:5). Forget it!

Keep these two essentials for a good marriage in mind. You must be both a good lover and a great forgiver.

A classic example of what to do when forgiving is the experience of former president Jimmy Carter. He once told reporters how he handled some personal injuries. "I went down the list in my mind of those whom I felt had hurt me and asked God to give them a special blessing."

This shows the bonus that goes with forgiveness, "pray for them." As a rinse, it purges the heart of bitterness.

Praise

Praise expedites rejuvenation. A pat on the back does more for cohesiveness than a knock on the head.

The dean of all major league umpires, Bill Klem, once told a newcomer to the profession that he should be married. Klem said, "When it seems all the world is against you—when fans boo and players criticize—that's the time you need someone to love and tell your troubles to."

Umpires are a microcosm of life, with daily flights of "boo birds" swirling around every person. A place of escape is needed and home should be that place. Not only should it be free from criticism, it should be a place of renewal. Those who live there should receive from you regular verbal "lovegrams."

"Judge not, and ye shall not be judged: condemn not, and ye shall not be condemned: forgive, and ye shall be forgiven" (Luke 6:37).

Take the initiative in being sure this is the attitude that prevails within the walls of your world. Be a pacesetter, a model. "... guide the house, give none occasion to the adversary to speak reproachfully" (1 Timothy 5:14). To guide means to lead. The best way to lead is by example.

Encouragement can be shared if you give each member of your household at least three positive perks a day. Find at least three things to compliment each day. Look for them. As your sensitivity grows, they will become more evident. Soon you won't have to look for them, and your expressions will become reflexive. It will set the mood for the entire family, making your home a positive environment.

Jonathan Edwards noted: "The ultimate goal is to treat something according to its true value." The value of a good wife is far above that of precious jewels, and frequent praise acknowledges her worth. Most people can go for a couple of days on one good compliment. Remember how good you felt the last time someone paid you a well-deserved compliment? Why not resolve to make someone feel good frequently? That someone should be your wife. What have you done or said to make her feel good lately?

Try praising your wife and children, even if it frightens them at first.

Be a "good finder." You won't find that word in your dictionary, however, there is magic in good finding. Good finding doesn't require flattery, just facts. Good finding makes two people feel good; the one finding the good and the one about whom the good is found.

An expressive good finder can overcome and eventually convert a faultfinder. Faultfinders are well defined in the dictionary as "calculated to confuse or entrap or entangle in argument marked by an inclination to stress faults and raise objections." It is unwise to engage in combat with faultfinders using their weapons. You will lose every time. Sincere good finders enrich relationships by accenting the best in others; when you find it, acknowledge it.

Some years ago an experiment with children clearly showed the importance of praise. A large group of children was divided into three groups. Care was taken to insure the groups were nearly equal in ability, average age, and sex. They were all given the same test.

The next day they were all assembled in one room for another test. Before the test, children in group one were called to the front of the room, praised for those parts of the test on which they had done well, and encouraged to do even better.

Children in group two were called to the front and criticized for the careless mistakes they had made.

Children in group three heard the praise and criticism, but no comment was made to them. They were completely ignored.

A new test was given, and this procedure was followed for four days. The progress of each group was recorded. The percentage of improvement for each group was:

>   Praised group .... 71 percent
>   Criticized group .... 20 percent
>   Ignored group .... 5 percent

This would indicate that praise encourages improvement. This principle holds true in a husband/wife relationship also. Conduct your own experiment and objectively observe the improvement. Keep it up, making it a lifetime experiment.

I have a friend in New York who is an exceptional artist. One characteristic I have noted about him is that he enjoys giving beauty to others. We should each be a verbal artist. You can find joy in giving the beauty of praise to others. Remember, "Flowers leave part of their fragrance in the hand that bestows them."

"All of us want to be needed, all of us wish to be admired," states Dr. Marcus Kline, psychologist and lecturer on human relations. "Most of us try to do good work, but how can we be sure we are needed, or are good workmen, or admirable companions, unless someone tells us so?"

You can make certain that those around you *know* they are loved and appreciated by being expressive and showing others that they and their deeds are not taken for granted. Every husband needs to work on this trait.

Lord Chesterfield, in one of his famous letters to his son, wrote, "Make other people like themselves a little better, my son, and I promise you they will like you very well."

Praise is a two-way thoroughfare. If you make sure traffic flows from you to others, you can be sure it will flow with equal volume toward you. You make it easy for people to like you by making them like themselves more. The best way to do this is to let them know the admirable qualities you see in them.

Always be truthful. Never be trite. To do so, you merely need to be sensitive. Verbalize your optimistic observations. By praising your partner, you indicate your appreciation.

Love

Love is elementary to closeness. To live together happily and harmoniously, there must be love. The word has suffered from such abuse and misuse that its true meaning is clouded. Often a model is needed to understand a principle. A coach will often walk through a play to help an athlete understand how to do it. A medical student will observe an experienced surgeon in order to learn how to perform an operation. A director will recite a line to enable an actor to comprehend what expression is needed. So love needs a model. A peerless one is given.

The Bible says, "Husbands, love your wives, even as Christ also loved the church, and gave himself for it" (Ephesians 5:25).

In no place does the Bible command the wife to love the husband. The husband is commanded to love his wife. Christ's relationship with His Church, His bride, is given as the prototype of the husband/wife relationship. Therefore, to understand how a husband should love his wife, study Christ's relationship with the Church. Observe and obey this example.

"Let this mind be in you, which was also in Christ Jesus: Who, being in the form of God, thought it not robbery to be

How to Be a Huggable Husband

equal with God: But made himself of no reputation, and took upon him the form of a servant, and was made in the likeness of men: And being found in fashion as a man, he humbled himself . . ." (Philippians 2:5–8).

In all of our relationships, we are to have the mind set of Christ. That means thinking like Christ. Establish that as your mental standard.

Two things stand out in this passage regarding Christ's attitude. First, His servant temperament is indicated. It resulted in Him humbling Himself willfully. It was not that He did not have the right, title, or position that might normally result in superiority. He *chose* to humble Himself. This is a choice open to every husband. It is a wise one, a practical practice. Love will prompt a person to do this.

A husband should never consider it beneath his dignity to help his wife with responsibilities normally considered hers. Cleaning the table, washing dishes, scrubbing toilet bowls, making the bed, or vacuuming the house should never be considered too menial for a husband. Doing them is an indirect way of saying, "I understand and love you. I support you." It is a way of letting a wife know she is the First Lady of her husband's kingdom. You show love by serving.

Jesus said, ". . . I am come that they might have life, and that they might have it more abundantly" (John 10:10).

Speaking in the supernatural realm, this text means Christ gives "super additives" to life. Jesus was full of joy, excitement, and surprises. Are you? Every husband should strive to be known as Mr. Excitement. Is that the way you are thought of? If you love as Christ loved, you will be. What "super additives" do you bring daily to your marriage? Love will motivate you to look for opportunities to serve and share.

Christ gave Himself for His Church. Love prompts a spirit of self-sacrifice. A servant temperament is a spirit of sacrifice. Test yourself regarding a servant temperament. Note how you react the next time someone treats you like a servant.

In some quarters, improper balance has been given to the husband's role. The fact that he is the head of the family causes some to minimize his self-sacrificing responsibility. Christ also was the head of the Church, yet He was her willing sacrifice. As the head, He gave Himself for His beloved bride.

"Let every one of us please his neighbor.... For even Christ pleased not himself..." (Romans 15:2, 3). Following Christ's example, look for ways to please your wife, not yourself. Make a list of things you might do that would please her, then start with number one. Should you do it? Can you do it? Why not do it? Do it! It is a way of saying "I love you." That is how Christ showed His love for us. Having started with number one, now move through your list. This can be fun, exciting, and gratifying. It can revolutionize your marriage.

Jesus said, "I will not leave you comfortless..." (John 14:18). Jesus provided for His beloved. Thus, love is seen to have deep concern for another's needs. A husband should be concerned about all of the needs of his wife: spiritual, social, economic, and physical. Are you looking after her comforts to the very best of your ability? Does she know you are concerned even beyond your capacity? Even if you can't provide for all of her comforts, she is comforted by knowing of your concern.

Put her comfort before your own. This is a beautiful way of indirectly saying, "I love you." Remember, your model is Christ and His love for His bride, the Church.

Provide an atmosphere in which she is comfortable. Never let her feel threatened or rivaled by another person. She is not only to be number one, she is to be the only one.

Allegedly Eve said to Adam, "Do you love me?"

To this he replied, "Who else?"

A wife deserves the comfort of knowing there is no one else. By virtue of being your wife, she is unique, one of a kind. A husband may have many females in his life, but only one wife. No other female should be allowed to threaten the role God has designed for her in the life of her husband. It is always improper and unfair to compare one's wife with any other female. Remember, your wife is unique. There is none other like her. Be attentive to your wife in various settings. Assume the responsibility of helping contribute to her comfort at all times. This gives a sense of stewardship and can be very fulfilling for a husband—and a wife.

Establish Goals

First Thessalonians 4:16, 17 speaks of Christ's ultimate plan for His Church. If you are to love as Christ loved, you need a sense of direction, a goal. When a husband and wife share a mutual goal, there is a willingness to pull together to reach it. The very process of striving for it brings the two closer together as one in intent and effort.

Christ's ultimate plan for His bride has established an understanding. If His goal for His Church had not been written, it might not be understood. Being known, it can be anticipated.

Husbands should take the initiative in establishing written goals for their marriage. Unwritten goals often become vague utopian dreams, less likely to be reached.

Start with your lifetime goals. What are they? This is not intended to be an experiment in cosmic clairvoyance. There is nothing magic about lifetime goals. They simply become guidelines, keeping us on a prescribed course. In this way your marriage can be a meaningful specific and not a wandering generality. Knowing where you are going will motivate you to plot the route for getting there.

Next discuss openly how you would like to live the next three years. These intermediate goals should be a major step toward your ultimate goal. They must not be a digression.

Now ask yourself a hard question: If you were to be killed in a freak accident six months from now, how would you like to live your remaining six months? That will give you a sense of immediacy. What would you like to squeeze into these six remaining months of life? Hopefully you are going to live a long time and fulfill your ultimate goals. This six-month perspective will motivate you to be sure you don't waste six months on your way to your ultimate goal.

The Bible does not tell us not to make plans for tomorrow, but rather to lay all plans for tomorrow on the altar of God (James 4:13, 14). Thus any goal established by a Christian becomes a statement of faith. In this way you are offering your life as a gift to God. Any plan not worthy of being offered to Him is not worthy of your life. Any plan worthy of life is worthy of being offered to Him for His blessings on it.

These four steps should be followed in developing your plans:

1. Define objectives
2. Build beliefs
3. Develop strengths
4. Evaluate progress

Few joys are comparable to that of setting a worthy goal and reaching it. As Christ planned for His bride, so there needs to be a plan for your marriage. It is a way of saying, "I love you like Christ loved His Church."

Emboss your life with love.

Refresh your understanding of the type of love you should have for your wife by reviewing the love Christ had for His bride. It is the original you are to copy, not a blurred cheap copy. Evidence the image of the original in the copy you show the world.

Peter spoke of the wife as being the weaker vessel. This refers to physical strength only. It does not hint of character, or male strength in response to temptation. The word *weakness* simply means she is more delicate. It does not allude to inferiority. An exquisite rose is delicately formed and easily injured.

One of the several characteristics of the Good Shepherd is that "he restoreth my soul." A husband should be observant to opportunities to restore his wife. Some spend more time restoring old cars than they do their wives.

Peter further noted that husbands and wives are heirs together. That is, both sexes occupy the same position and rank in relationship to Christ. They are clearly on an equal spiritual plane. "... there is neither male nor female: for ye are all one in Christ Jesus" (Galatians 3:28).

The expression heirs together literally means joint heirs. Joint heirs own all things equally together. What belongs to one belongs to both. They are co-equal. This is the pattern that must be followed in all aspects of the marriage relationship. This is love.

We are also spoken of as being joint heirs with Christ (*see* Romans 8:17). That means what is His is ours when ours is also His. Being a joint heir means owning all things co-equally. When that outlook is shared and enjoyed by a couple in their role as husband and wife, there is strength and sweetness in the marriage.

When our beloved daughter Lynn was about to become the wife of Dr. Roger Hill, they discussed their proposed new life together. She confided in him her financial position. He complimented her and then added, "Lynn, all that I have is yours." That is a summary of love. Make sure it prevails in all of life.

5

Love Her, Lover

A marriage can be holy wedlock or an unholy deadlock. The primary key is the husband. As God's intended imitator, he can unlock the storehouse of happiness or keep the family locked in the rubble of heartache.

The importance of his role in the family is revealed in his title—husband—the word meaning "the band of the house." This usage is given meaning when considered in light of a fall harvest. The shocks or bundles of grain had a band put around them to hold them together. In this frame of reference, the head of the home became known as the "house band," or husband.

Marriage is the only sentence that can be suspended for *bad* behavior. The objective in marriage is not to suspend it, but to sustain it. The husband has more to do with the behavioral mood of the family than any other member. His very presence often changes the mood in a room when he enters. If the wife, and to a lesser extent the children, reflect his image, he can gain a glimpse of that image by observing their reaction to his action.

Authority and Submission

A marriage does not have to be a conjugal Vietnam, resulting in a stalemate. Marriage can be a pleasant and profitable venture. The terms of the peace agreement are well-defined in the Bible. Most men can quote the essence of Ephesians 5:22, 23, which they capsulate in the word *submit*.

> Wives, submit yourselves unto your own husbands, as unto the Lord. For the husband is the head of the wife, even as Christ is the head of the church: and he is the saviour of the body.

Without stammering, most husbands can state, "Submit unto your own husbands." Often an air of superiority arises from the authority given the male by this text. A dictatorial posture is assumed and asserted because of these verses.

Strangely, there seems to be a convenient nuptial amnesia regarding the associated verses of Ephesians 5:25, 28.

> Husbands, love your wives, even as Christ also loved the church, and gave himself for it. . . . So ought men to love their wives as their own bodies. He that loveth his wife loveth himself.

That gets down to the basic nitty and fundamental gritty of the husband's role. For the man, this is where accountable action starts.

The Scripture commands the wife to submit to the husband. That is her biblical responsibility. She is accountable and answerable for that. Many of them will ultimately be greatly rewarded for complying with the command, even in obeying a carnal husband. The wife is responsible for this submission, not the husband. Therefore he should never try to force or coerce her submission. That results in rebellious suppression, not refreshing submission. The response intended from the wife is never achieved by physical force or Bible quoting.

How is it achieved? Only through love. Often it is achieved by the wife's overwhelming love for Christ, which prompts her to obey His Word even in light of masculine mauling and manipulation.

Submission results more readily when the love of Christ is coupled with that of a loving husband. As the husband is not commanded to submit to the wife, even so the wife is not commanded to love her husband. It is the husband who is *commanded* to love the wife. It is not subtly suggested, it is strategically stated—*do it.*

God, knowing a woman's makeup because He designed her, knows she does not respond as well to a command as she does to love. Therefore, He offers man the best and most effective implement to achieve the desired end—love. Force can never do what love can do. Solomon noted the power of love: "Many waters cannot quench love, neither can the floods drown it . . ." (Song of Solomon 8:7).

God, the Creator, knows the only way to obtain a woman's love is by love. Hence, He instructs man to love her, not to lord over her.

Avoid Bitterness

The husband is commanded to love his wife again in Colossians 3:19: "Husbands, love your wives, and be not bitter against them."

Therein is contained a positive and a negative. First the negative: Be not bitter against them. Bitterness toward a woman who has given up her all to become a man's second self is grossly wrong. Bitterness, whether expressed in surly silence or sharp speech, is never right. Even if a wife resists and resents her God-given role, there is no room for bitter-

Love Her, Lover

ness on behalf of the husband. An aid in avoiding it is recorded in Ephesians 4:31, 32:

> Let all bitterness, and wrath, and anger, and clamour, and evil speaking, be put away from you, with all malice. And be ye kind one to another, tenderhearted, forgiving one another, even as God for Christ's sake hath forgiven you.

God not only gives us instructions regarding forgiving, He also cites an example. Any time a husband finds it hard to forgive his wife, he is encouraged to remember how greatly Christ loved him in order to achieve his forgiveness. Christ gave Himself for us. In like manner, the husband is urged to be willing to give his life for his wife. The husband who expresses and manifests this life-giving type of love will find his wife willing to fulfill her role for such a loving one.

Xenophon relates that when Cyrus took captive a young Armenian prince and his beautiful wife, they were brought before a tribunal to receive their sentences. Cyrus asked the young prince what he would give to be reinstated to his kingdom. The prince declared that he valued his crown and his liberty very little, compared to his love for his bride. He implored the noble conqueror to restore his beloved wife to her former dignity and possessions, offering his life in payment for such a privilege.

Cyrus was so moved by this love that he released the two together.

Each was lavish in praise of Cyrus. Later the young prince inquired of his wife, "What think ye of Cyrus?"

She replied, "I did not observe him."

"Not observe him!" exclaimed her husband in amazement. "Upon whom then was your attention fixed?"

She responded, "Upon that dear and generous man who declared his readiness to purchase my liberty at the expense of his life."

Christ loved His bride, the Church, and gave Himself for it. Likewise, the husband is to be willing to give himself for his wife. That is the positive affirmation of Colossians 3:19.

Selfless Love

Do you love your wife? Do you love her with a self-giving love? The inquiry is not, "Do you do nice things for her?" Nor is it, "Do you whisper sweet things to her?" The question relates to giving yourself to and for her.

Christ's love for us is Exhibit A of how we are to love each other. He loves sacrificially.

There were three Greek words commonly used for love. Our language is not as precise, and this causes a lack of comprehension of love's meaning.

One of the words was *eros*. Our word erotic comes from it. It is the word that describes physical attraction between two persons, which is good and proper in marriage.

The second is *phileo*. This is a reference to brotherly love—friendship is the closest word in the English language. This also is needed in marriage. Your wife wants to be your best friend. Don't shut her out. Don't ever injure a friend.

The third word for love is *agape*. This means love measured by sacrifice. It is selfless love, the prototype of which is Christ's love for us. He loves us because it is His nature. It is not our virtue or merit that prompts His love. This type of love is needed between husband and wife.

All three forms of love are needed in marriage. Dangers arise when imbalance occurs. If one of the three is stressed and the others neglected, misunderstanding can occur. Likewise, if one of the three is left out, the other two are weakened, and suspicion results.

Love produces trust and eliminates rivalry. When two persons can lovingly accept each other as they are, then each can confidently assume his rightful role without resentment. A classic illustration of this is the Godhead. Each member of the Trinity is co-equal to the other. Yet each has a different primary manifestation. We are urged to:

> Let this mind be in you, which was also in Christ Jesus: Who, being in the form of God, thought it not robbery to be equal with God: But made himself of no reputation, and took upon him the form of a servant, and was made in the likeness of men.
>
> Philippians 2:5–7

So confident was the Son of His equality with the Father and the Spirit that He lovingly humbled Himself and assumed the needful form of a servant. There is no competitiveness between people who accept each other as equals. Neither is there any reluctance to humbly accept diverse roles. There is no suspicion of motives when love prevails. A confidence that each complements and completes the other is dominant. Equals do not mind being distinct and different.

A man cannot love his wife too much. Christ loved the Church so much that He cared for its spiritual needs. Every individual is born with an innate desire to worship.

This trait is evidently more dominant in the female than in the male. The female who sees her husband humble himself before God finds it easier to submit to him. The wife who worships with a husband who submits to the authority over him complies with her role more readily. A husband who resists the worship of God will be resented as one demanding respect for his authority without respecting God's authority.

"Christ is the head of every man, the head of the woman is her husband, and the Head of Christ is God" (*see* 1 Corinthians 11:3).

Christ, a member of the Godhead, is equal with the Father. Yet in His earthly role, He became subject to the Father. Thus, the divine order is structured:

> God the Father, Jehovah
> God the Son, Jesus Christ
> Man, the husband
> Woman, the wife
> Children

As Christ, though the Father's equal, is subject to Him, even so the wife, who is equal to her husband, is subject to him. Any man who will not respond to the authority over him makes it hard for those under his authority to submit.

Any husband and wife who destroy this order and violate God's design can expect their children to rebel against their authority. All authority is resented by a child who lives with a parent or parents who try to exercise authority without submitting to authority. A good example is always an ideal teaching tool.

Ordered Order

To prevent disorder and chaos in any functioning unit, someone must assume major responsibilities, make decisions, and direct activities. Any successful business or organization recognizes this need. Yet frequently families ignore the principle of leadership and therefore do not experience the harmony and peace God meant them to enjoy. Since the family is the basic unit of society, its stability will determine not only the security and happiness of its members, but also the strength of the nation. Stability for both home and nation depends on recognizing the man as head of the family.

Some people think marriage is a 50-50 deal, but it is not. It requires 100 percent from each partner, each having a role that demands his all. Each role is judged in terms of its function and cannot operate efficiently without the other. A husband and wife complement each other in much the same way as a lock and key go together—either is incomplete without the other.

A man tends to differ from a woman in his interests, thinking, and abilities, as well as in his body. These distinctions make him the wife's complement, but they do not make him inferior or superior. Neither man nor woman has cause for boasting, and neither needs to fret about having an inferior position.

The roles of husband and wife could be compared to the

offices of president and vice-president of an organization. Each party understands, on acceptance of the position, that each office carries with it heavy responsibilities. Since the policies are clearly established, there is never any doubt about who is the president. However, the president's success depends on the vice-president's help in carrying out the policies. When new decisions have to be made, the president may consult with the vice-president for advice, but he assumes responsibility for the final decision.

Once a policy is decided, they work together as a team to carry it out. The president may, if he chooses, delegate some of his authority to the vice-president. When the president is gone, he can trust the vice-president to carry on as if he were there. In this relationship, they share a oneness, good communication, emotional peace, and security, provided the vice-president is not struggling to gain control of the organization!

God meant the roles of men and women to be different. After all, He made them male and female, not unisex. This difference is not only physical, but also emotional and temperamental. Masculine traits include the ability to see the overall picture in a situation and to be firm and decisive when solving problems. Womanly traits include the ability to see the details of a situation and to contribute valuable insights based on a compassionate, sensitive nature.

For instance, as you prepare for a business party, your wife may be caught up in the details of the party preparation, or how to prevent Mrs. X from offending Mrs. Y. You may be thinking in terms of how the party will contribute to your business success for the coming year. By using your respective natural talents, you will be able to work together as a team.

If you do not recognize that God designed you and your wife to complement each other, you may try to force your wife to act and respond to life as you do. Should you succeed, she would have to switch to the masculine role of being the initiator, abandoning her feminine responsibilities. If you recognize, however, that by nature your roles are different, you can develop your masculine traits and become a truly masculine man.

Male-female responses A medical doctor in New Orleans was the first to share a fundamental difference in the male and female with me. She noted that when God made us male and female, He did a superb job of diversification. Responses by the two to the same situation or stimuli are completely different.

The male was created to operate by logic or reason. When any subject is considered, it is looked at from a viewpoint of logic and reason. This is good, but it is not all good. Therefore, He created woman.

The female was created to operate intuitively, with greater depth of feeling. There are some commercials that take this into account. They say, "She is a woman, she feels more deeply." The same subject, approached analytically and candidly, will be considered with far more feeling by the female. This is good, but it is not all good.

The two goods together are totally good. The husband brings his logic and reasoning ability and the wife her intuition and feeling, and they two become one in a new structured mentality and emotional manner. Each fulfills the other.

It must be added hastily that this does not mean to imply that the male has no feelings, any more than it is to suggest that the female has no logic. Each certainly has the other, but the degree with which each is held is the difference.

Ignorance of this elemental insight or obstinacy regarding it causes many problems. Frequently a husband will crush, insult, hurt, and injure his wife unwittingly and unintentionally. It is done by trying to treat her like one of the fellows. She has greater depth of feeling and responds with fuller feeling. Don't ever criticize a woman for being emotional. That is a beautiful part of her makeup. It's a phase of the male psyche that is only properly developed by the female, who enhances it in her husband.

This variance may be observed when watching television. The husband is thinking, "This is a super story. . . . that is a great stage prop. . . . those are excellent lighting effects. . . . the characters all put themselves into their lines." At that moment, he looks at his wife and sees a tear rolling down her cheek. She is feeling *with* the characters. She shares their plight emotionally.

My wife is not a hyper-emotional person, but she is normal. Soon after we married, she walked through the room, where I was seated. (Note I said, "the room." We only had one.) I said, "Honey, hand me that magazine on the table." Seconds later I noticed she had a tear rolling down her cheek. Hastily I asked what was wrong.

She replied, "You didn't say please."

Wow! I meant please—but I didn't say it. She and I were both reared in homes where that was said. When I had neglected to say it, I projected the image of a brute to my new bride. My wife is not a weepy woman, but those early tears in our marriage prompted me to respect her as a sensibly sensitive person.

Emotions vary Somewhere I read an impressive article by another female doctor. The thesis had to do with a perfectly normal woman. In essence, the perfectly normal woman has varying emotional moods. A wise husband realizes this and responds accordingly. There is a time when she is emotionally up and the world is her apple. Try as he may, the male can't get this high. She is on top of the world. At another time, she is in an emotional slump. When she is down, she is down. When a loving husband detects this, he extends a little more loving effort to help her up emotionally and waits patiently for her response.

Ideally a responsive wife recognizes this and lovingly extends an effort to be more "up" than she would otherwise. Even at her best during this time, she will not be her most radiant self.

Before any male becomes critical of this fact, he would do

well to observe his own mood cycle. Though it is not as distinct as the female's, it is just as definite. He, too, has low times.

The man who really loves his wife will capitalize on all these natural traits. Her love flows more freely toward one who allows his love to flow freely to God. A woman takes great pride in being able to sit beside the man she loves in worship of God, who authored love. The time spent together in worship is an enhancement to the total marriage.

Forgiveness

With Christ's love for the Church as a model, forgiveness becomes an important factor in marriage. A central theme in the Cross of Calvary, which epitomizes love, is forgiveness. Holding a grudge and refusing to forgive result in estrangement. Forgiveness is made easy by comparing what you are forgiving with what He has forgiven. If a holy supernatural God will forgive finite fumbling persons, surely we can forgive each other. Do not ever be too proud to say, "I am sorry" or "Please forgive me."

"For if ye forgive men their trespasses, your heavenly Father will also forgive you: But if ye forgive not men their trespasses, neither will your Father forgive your trespasses" (Matthew 6:14, 15).

> He that will not forgive,
> remains unforgiven
> because he is unforgivable.

Jesus has taught us to pray, "And forgive us our debts, as we forgive our debtors" (Matthew 6:12). "And when ye stand praying, forgive, if ye have ought against any: that your Father also which is in heaven may forgive you your trespasses" (Mark 11:25).

We should live, "Forbearing one another, and forgiving one another, if any man have a quarrel against any: even as Christ forgave you, so also do ye" (Colossians 3:13).

Bitterness associated with happenings can only be flushed by forgiveness. It is therapeutically good because

> Bitterness does more harm
> To the vessel in which it is stored,
> Than to the one on which it is poured.

No wife can be manipulated to respond favorably physically to a person who is known to be emotionally bitter. If you love her, forgive and seek forgiveness.

Forgiveness is invariably needed on our own behalf. Therefore, give it readily. A lack of domestic tranquility is seen as a hindrance to prayer. The husband should be the aggressor in establishing and maintaining good domestic relations in order "that your prayers be not hindered" (*see* 1 Peter 3:7).

Not only does a person often need the forgiveness of his mate, but also of his Master. To obtain it, first forgive others and then practice 1 John 1:9: "If we confess our sins, he is faithful and just to forgive us our sins, and to cleanse us from all unrighteousness."

Forfeiting One's Rights

With Christ serving as his example, a man must be willing to sacrifice some of his rights for his wife. Christ gave up His rights to preserve ours. A loving husband is more concerned with his responsibilities than with his rights. It is his responsibility to exercise authority. The authority exercised is not his own, but that of Christ.

Humble Authority

He should exercise authority in humility.

This is not his right, but his duty. As such, he should praise his wife. Proverbs 31:10–31 is a peerless passage of praise due to women.

Authority should never be exercised harshly. Colossians 3:19 warns against this improper attitude.

Humility is a vital virtue in a man. Christ manifested it graphically in washing the feet of the disciples (John 13:3–5).

In like manner, the husband should evidence his love for his wife.

Tell Her You Love Her

In speaking to the Dallas Cowboys, I urged them to tell their wives of their love. One of their big linemen came up later and, looking down on my little 6′5″ frame, said, "Why do I need to tell her again that I love her? I told her that when I married her." I urged him to try it anyway. The next day when I saw him, he grinned and said, "That's the best advice anyone has given me in a long time."

Love her, lover!

6

The Cost of Communicating

"Have I reached the party to whom I am speaking?"

A noted female comedian impersonating a telephone operator has made that humorous line popular. The irony of it is many people do *not* reach the person to whom they are speaking. Talking, saying something, and hearing may all come short of communicating—reaching people.

Experts in the field of communications estimate that 85 percent of one's income depends upon communication skills—talking and listening.

It is impossible to estimate what percentage of a happy

marriage is dependent upon the ability of a couple to communicate. Sending and receiving messages bring a couple together in the beginning of a romance. It is essential to continue the process, if the romance is to prosper. Ask yourself:

1. Can I communicate better this year than last?
2. What have I read during the last year to help me improve my ability to communicate?
3. How good am I at converting people to my way of thinking?
4. Can I express my thoughts clearly?
5. Am I a good listener?

Listen

Listening is a vital virtue in communication. The failure to do so can result in confusion. An illustration of this is the dad who was seated comfortably in his favorite chair, reading the sports page. One of his young children walked in and said, "Dad, guess what? Mom says she wants to be cremated."

The dad's droll response was, "Okay, tell her to get her coat and purse and let's go."

"Minds are like parachutes: they only work when they are open," said Lord Thomas Robert DeWar. Keeping an open ear and open mind are strategic parts of communicating. Your mate's awareness of being heard gives her a sense of importance.

There are numerous family-affecting decisions that ultimately have to be made by one person, the husband. He should process all input in reaching a conclusion. The wife should be confident that though her opinion might not determine the decision, it will influence it. Share.

"A wise man will hear, and will increase learning; and a man of understanding shall attain unto wise counsels" (Proverbs 1:5).

A British newspaper once carried this gossip item, which

reveals a human trait. "James McNeill Whistler and Oscar Wilde were seen yesterday at Brighton, talking as usual about themselves."

Whistler clipped the item and mailed it to Wilde with this note: "I wish the reporters would be accurate. If I remember, Oscar, we were talking about me."

To which Wilde sent the following telegram in reply: "It is true, Jimmie, we were talking about you, but I was thinking of myself!"

To avoid the hazard posed by the spirit indicated in that humorous interchange—*listen.*

If you are a good listener, you will have good recall. People like to think that what they say is of enough importance to be remembered. The ability to recall and repeat flatters the person whose statement you relate.

A classic case of poor listening is illustrated by this apocryphal story.

A young man wrote his girlfriend: "I know I proposed to you last night, but I forgot whether you said yes or no."

The quick-witted young woman responded: "Thank you for writing. I knew I refused someone's proposal last night, but could not remember whose."

If you listen well, you will be able to recall equally well. It indicates to others that not only what they say is of importance to you, but what they are is important.

Silence

Sir Oliver Wendell Holmes commented, "Talking is very much like playing on the harp. There is as much in laying the hand on the strings to stop their vibrations as in twanging them to bring out the music."

Silence can be an important part of communication. It can mean, "I've got a problem I don't want to burden you with. Give me a little time to work it out." Conversely, it can be saying, "I am mad at you, and I am going to punish you by shutting you out."

Silence should never be used punitively. The silent treatment is a heartless, cruel way of cutting all lines of logic. "Wherefore, my beloved brethren, let every man be swift to hear, slow to speak, slow to wrath" (James 1:19).

The average person does not use or readily understand more than 10 percent of the 600,000 words in the English language. The abuse and misuse of the 10 percent they do know cause more problems than the lack of comprehension of the other 90 percent.

As Job said, "How forcible are right words! . . ." (Job 6:25). Words are weapons. Choose the right weapons, and use them sparingly. "He that hath knowledge spareth his words: and a man of understanding is of an excellent spirit" (Proverbs 17:27).

The law of diminishing returns takes over if a person talks too much. Words lose their vitality when spoken in volume—balance is needed. To use the silent treatment or to flood the market of hearing with an overabundance of words creates imbalance. When you can improve on silence, speak. Silence is golden if used in love, but speech is lethal to love if misused. Balance is essential.

If you offend your mate, apologize without hesitation. It shows your more practical side, while refusal to do so shows obstinacy and impudence. Every person has a need to apologize—more often than they imagine.

"For in many things we offend all. If any man offend not in word, the same is a perfect man, and able also to bridle the whole body" (James 3:2).

When it is appropriate, say it: "I am sorry. I apologize." Love motivates such candor. Love is stimulated by such sincerity.

Gracious Speech

"Let your speech be alway with grace, seasoned with salt, that ye may know how ye ought to answer every man" (Colossians 4:6)—and particularly your mate.

Salt adds taste to food; grace adds flavor to speech. Salt is a preservative. Speech that issues out of a nature of grace preserves good relations between husbands and wives. One elemental definition of grace is unmerited favor. Therefore, we must not be goaded into a harsh response simply because someone asked for it. Perhaps they do not deserve a kind response, but that is all the more reason to give one. "Grace is to speech what color is to art."

"The words of a wise man's mouth are gracious; but the lips of a fool will swallow up himself" (Ecclesiastes 10:12).

Kind Speech

Kindness is a garnish similar to grace. It is impossible for one person to have an argument—two are required. Therefore, a cardinal rule of marriage is that both husband and wife should *never* get upset at the same time. If one sees the other angry, that should be a signal for pleasant words. "Pleasant words are as an honeycomb, sweet to the soul, and health to the bones" (Proverbs 16:24).

A little honey never hurt anyone. For centuries this delicious food has been known to taste good and have medicinal quality. For these reasons, the Psalmist likens the use of pleasant words to a honeycomb. Mentally picture the words you intend to use in a given situation. Compare their likeness to a honeycomb. It never hurts to sweet-talk your mate, even in the most casual conversation. If talking to you is a pleasant experience, you will be amazed how the channels of communication will open. To make your speech more appetizing: avoid bitter, caustic comments; respond politely, even if hostilely rebuffed; show poise; be patient. If the channels of communication are impaired, repair them with pleasant words.

We need understanding, knowledge, love, and compassion for each other in order to communicate constructively. These qualities represent our greatest needs, consequently they are our greatest opportunity.

The Bible advocates that we speak the truth in love. Not

only should we speak the truth, but our speech should always be motivated by love. This implies that love will sometimes motivate us *not* to speak, because in doing so we might injure someone. The capacity to keep a confidence is important in communication.

Some things must be sub rosa. A romantic tale lies behind that phrase. According to Greek mythology, the god of silence, Harpocrates, stumbled upon Venus, the goddess of love, involved in one of her amorous adventures.

Cupid, the son of Venus, came along at the same time. By making a gift of a rose to Harpocrates, he received a pledge of secrecy. Since that time, the rose has become the symbol of silence.

During the Renaissance and later during the rule of the prerevolutionary kings of France, the rose was a favorite decoration among architects. It was often sculpted or painted on the ceilings or walls of dining and drawing rooms where diplomats gathered. The implication was that the matters to be discussed were "under the rose," that is, confidential.

When our children were young, we would often put a single rose on the dining table when we were to have a confidential family share time. Every person needs to know there is a sub rosa time of conversation.

Desire Determines Effectiveness

You can communicate, if you want to. No matter how estranged or entangled relations may become, two persons can communicate if they really *want* to. In Rome, Italy, I needed to get from the Colosseum to Leonardo da Vinci Airport. The man responsible for my transportation spoke little English, and I no Italian. He wanted to do what I wanted done because he makes a living transporting people. I wanted to get to the airport because I didn't want to miss my flight home. We both really wanted to communicate. We had very little basis on which to communicate, other than a desire to do so. This alone stimulated us through patient and persistent pursuit of understanding. It worked—we got through to each other. He understood where I wanted to go, and I understood what it would cost. Ideas were conveyed despite the language barrier. If two people who do not even speak the same language can relate to each other simply because they want to, surely a husband and wife who want to can. Obstinacy, not ignorance, is the only obstacle. A real desire to communicate can remove this roadblock to reason.

Do you remember your courtship? Talk came easy then. It was so easy that it might even be embarrassing to compare it with the present. Then you *wanted* to talk. The fuller discovery of each other's world was a driving desire. You appeared to understand each other. There was an openness. It was reassuring to know you had found someone who understood you, someone you wanted to understand. That drew you together as you talked about personal things, intimate matters, essentials. It made you feel good. You were encouraged by the fact that evidently your beloved was made to feel good because of being understood.

That same sensation can be maintained. If it has deteriorated, it must be reactivated. Talk! Talk does not hurt or injure, but reveals and explores the continuing world of your mate. Let your beloved into your world. An insatiable need to be let in to your world exists in your mate. When interest is shown in your mate's interest, it activates interest in you. Ask questions, express enthusiasm, pay compliments, and lavish love verbally on your partner.

Understanding

"My husband doesn't understand me. I've met someone who does." That basically means, "I have met a person who will talk to me and listen to me." Often this mere talk deteriorates to sexual unfaithfulness. Where there is freedom of verbal expression between a couple, seldom does sexual promiscuity occur. Every person seeks to be understood. Make every possible effort to understand and be understood by being understanding. If one's mate is drawn to another by understanding, he or she can be drawn back the same way.

As a counterpart to this, do not be drawn away from your mate because some other person seems to understand you. Often this innocent interest becomes complicated carnality. It makes a person feel good to be understood, and everyone likes to feel good. However, the end product must be considered, namely, who is going to be hurt. When there is a triangle, an average of sixteen people are injured. It is reasonable, then, to avoid inflicting pain on sixteen others by avoiding selfish pleasure. Count the cost of counterfeit communication.

To avoid this, start at the point of origin. Don't let your words suggest attitudes that will precipitate adulterous actions. Don't flirt with temptation. Temptation has far more seductive power than the average person has restraint.

"And the tongue is a fire, a world of iniquity: so is the tongue among our members, that it defileth the whole body, and setteth on fire the course of nature; and it is set on fire of hell" (James 3:6).

The tongue is represented as the kindling, one's physical nature is the combustible, and the igniting is done by hell. The end result of promiscuity is painful. If we play with fire, we can expect to be burned. We can avoid carnal combustibility by abstaining from cultivated carnal communication. We should never play around the perimeter of the whirlpool of worldly words. The suction is too strong to struggle against too long. It can only pull a person down. Know the result before you wade in the water.

Judge Not

Your mate may be reluctant to try communicating with you because of:

1. Fear of being judged. Consistent criticism of every comment prompts people to simply quit commenting.
2. Fear of an avalanche of advice. Most people will ask for

advice when they want it. Helpful sharing of principles is advantageous, but constant instruction is insulting to one's intellect.

Marriage is not a license to suppress free speech. Both parties have the right to be heard. One husband commented, "Whenever my wife and I have a misunderstanding, we just sit down quietly and straighten me out." Often talking a thing out means "Let's talk until you accept my position."

Different Perspectives

Basic differences in the male-female makeup must be remembered in order to send and receive messages. The male uses logic and reason as his basic *modus operandi*, and the female uses her intuitive and sensory capacity. When a subject is discussed, each must endeavor to cross over to the other's viewpoint to establish a basis of mutual comprehension. This is not capitulation; it is concern for good communication.

This basic difference in thought patterns can further be developed as follows. Note the contrasts.

1. ***Male***   He has a theoretical mind. He is interested in theory and philosophy and talks about principles.
Female   She is more person centered. Her desire is to know to whom certain principles apply—who is involved, rather than what.
2. ***Male***   He expresses generalities. A day can be summed up in a sentence. It is not his intent to omit or forget, but simply to speak summarily.
Female   She thinks in details. She has no desire to bore with finite facts, she just reflects her nature and ability to retain interest in minutiae. There is no intent to bore with details, but simply to inform and share.
3. ***Male***   He speaks to communicate information. Facts are his forte. There is little emotion in his relating facts, and he has a hard time understanding why anyone would be emotionally involved in mere information.
Female   She desires to express emotions. Her depth of

feeling prompts her to often be dismayed that others might not feel as she does about a matter. She finds emotional release in sharing.

4. **Male** He often uses indirect expression in preference to direct expression. A hug, kiss, a look, or a caress is most often his way of saying, "I love you" without words.

Female She most often prefers direct expression in addition to indirect expression. She wants to hear those three little words "I love you" in advance of or in addition to actions intended to convey the idea.

To carry on and cultivate good husband-wife communications, the following points should be remembered:

Conversation is a means of conveying ideas as well as emotions. When one party is merely sharing ideas and the other emotions, conflict can occur if each is not understanding of the different perspective. In conversation, each person is pulled in two different directions: one is to develop a line of logic based on facts; the other is to satisfy emotional needs. Neither should be overlooked. Logic alone cannot be used to convey ideas to one's mate. A feeling of cooperativeness must be developed. Courtesy is the best catalyst to cooperation.

Respect for the other person's facts is important. Respect for their feelings is more strategic. Disrespect for facts and feelings results in a resistant mind. Resistant minds cannot be reached with reason, and that is why we must listen to others' ideas and put ourselves in our mate's position. Would what is being said encourage cooperation and diminish antagonism or not? You can be sensitized by listening to the emotions between the lines.

Always be willing to accept that which seems to be irrelevant and explore its purpose. Do not insist that everything has to be relevant. This can be very irritating. There are two kinds of relevancies: logical relevancy and emotional relevancy. Both of these must be considered when transmitting an idea. One must be flexible and patient enough to listen and endeavor to comprehend not only what is being said but why. The relevance of a remark depends largely on the personal purpose of the remark.

Low-structured questions help to draw out information and emotions. Questions that open the opportunity for talk about a topic, rather than merely a recitation of facts, are helpful. Set the mind in motion and conversation follows. Low-structured or general questions are advantageous in getting a general idea of one's line of thought, ascertaining insights you might not have considered asking about specifically, uncovering feelings that might hide behind a specific question, and drawing the other person into more active discussion. Don't just think your own thoughts—listen for the emotional expression contained in those of your wife.

Feel, Felt, Found

The idea of traversing a gap in agreement is a challenging one. One approach has been described as the "feel, felt, found" technique. It goes:

I know how you *feel*,
   I *felt* that way, too,
      until I *found*. . . .

This approach involves empathy with the person. It expresses understanding—"I *know* how you feel." Then it moves to association—"I felt that way, *too*." It concludes with an admission of having changed one's own posture because of further and fuller insight—"I *found*."

Understanding, association, and information are three assets in relating. All three are involved in this approach. There is no talking down to anyone and no pretentious personal superiority boasted. The approach is that of a friend talking with a friend about a path both have used. The intent is to arrive at the same destination in agreement.

7

You Determine Your Attitude

It's your life, given you by a loving Creator, God. Not even He, however, can or will determine your attitude.

God gives you the breath of life, energy for work, years in which to make decisions, and a mind with which to make them. He does much for us, but there is one thing He will not do for us: He will not make our decisions for us. If He did, we would only be marionettes dangling on divine strings.

Not only will He not make decisions for us, He won't let anybody determine our attitudes for us. We are free to choose. God leads us, friends impress us, circumstances influence us, and heredity impacts us, but only *we* determine our attitude.

Joy is an attitude. You are free to choose it or reject it. It isn't an involuntary reflex or an emotion—joy is an attitude. It is always an option you are free to choose. Hence, you can be joyous, if you choose to be. Of course, you don't have to choose joy. You can choose its opposite—gloom.

With gloom, you can run off even the most devout friend. You can ruin the happiest occasion, spoil the most delightful gathering, and dampen the cheeriest of spirits with a good dose of gloom.

Attitudes are more important than facts. You may not be able to change certain facts, but you can change your attitude. Facts can influence your attitude; your attitude can influence facts; facts and attitude are perpetually locked in mortal combat. Facts can get you down. Your attitude can enable you to overcome even evil (facts) with good (attitude).

The fact may be that your relationship is not good. Before you can do anything about that, you must make sure your attitude is good.

You can resolve to have a particular mind set. That is, you can conclude that regardless of what facts may prevail, your attitude will always be fixed. This will give you a consistent perspective from which to react. A commendable fixed attitude is *joy*. Inexhaustible joy rejuvenates relationships.

Joy is a prominent theme in Scripture. Carpet the corridors of your mind with Scripture, then every thought that runs through your mind will be conditioned by Scripture. What the Silicon Valley is to the field of technology, Scripture is to thought.

Reading the many passages in the Bible pertaining to joy is a thrilling undertaking. It becomes immediately apparent that the Lord desires you to have joy and to express it. In the Bible, joy showed up in the most unusual places. Paul had it while in jail. The hunted disciples were characterized by joy after the Resurrection, for Christ had promised them in their hour of grief that their sorrow would be turned to joy. In a time of affliction and great poverty, the church in Jerusalem demonstrated joy. James appealed to persons to express their joy even in times of great testing. Peter spoke of having unspeakable joy. John encouraged us to be full of joy.

In a world where someone has pulled the plug on joy, it is still possible to have it.

What Is Joy?

Joy is that unmistakable quality that reveals itself regardless of circumstances.

Ralph was so far below the poverty level, he had never heard of it. Food was scarce, clothing limited, and housing inadequate. Yet, joy abounded. As a child I enjoyed listening to him whistle. I've never known a sad or mad person to whistle. A glow came from Ralph's face even when the pain of death was in his body. He said, "I have the joy of the Lord in my heart."

When Faye came to see me, she had less than a month to live. She had just been told by her doctor. She came to ask, "What can I expect dying to be like? And what will heaven be like?"

I told her as best as I could. Then she said, "I have only a month to live, but even this fatal disease isn't going to rob me of the joy of these days."

It didn't. Right up until the time she slipped into her final coma, she had peace that passes understanding—great joy.

At the peak of his outstanding pro career, Bill suffered a knee injury. The words sent a shudder through strong athletes. It became immediately apparent that Bill's career was over. He said, "This knee injury has robbed me of the right to play, but I won't let it steal my joy of life."

It didn't. As a result, his joy became so contagious that others caught it.

Frank's business partner betrayed and robbed him. He was left with one option. Having just lost everything, the heartbreak of bankruptcy and its associated embarrassment were inevitable.

You Determine Your Attitude

"I've lost my fortune," he said, "but I will not lose my joy." He didn't. His resilient spirit and ingenuity enabled him to start over and later pay off all debts, even though they were legally absolved.

Aunt Terry was broken in body but not spirit. Age had robbed her of much of her sight and most of her strength, but not her joy. Even when she became slow of body and mind, reflexive joy still showed through. Her indomitable joy was not overcome by poverty, defeated by uncertainty, dispelled by loneliness. or dissipated by age. When anyone was down, she was always good for a lift. She lifted more spirits than an elevator has lifted persons.

He was known as "the world's strongest man." Paul Anderson thrilled millions with his weight-lifting feats, until a near-fatal illness requiring a kidney transplant stripped him of his strength. Having lost much weight and barely able to walk with a cane and the aid of his wife, Paul spoke. As he leaned on the podium for support, the frail frame of this great man of strength trembled. He gasped for breath to speak of the joy he had in the Lord.

Add all these personal qualities up as a subtotal. Now add to them the biblical meaning of the word joy. It means pleasure, delight, and happiness with a spirit of thankfulness. Joy has nothing to do with externals. Internals have everything to do with it. Joy is all this and more.

Joy is composure resulting from confidence that God is in control.

Joy is an awareness that the One in control is loving, gracious, kind, and compassionate.

Joy is sensitivity to the compassionate Creator's knowledge of all needs.

Joy is the belief that this loving and knowing God who is in control is worthy of trust. This being true, there is reason for joy.

In the beautiful story of African life entitled *Cry, the Beloved Country*, Kumalo, the village priest who had endured great suffering, had a conversation with Father Vincent. Kumalo said, "It seems that God has turned from me."

Father Vincent wisely responded, "That may seem to happen, but it does not happen. Never, never does it happen."

Joy knows that God never, never turns His back. He did it once and only once, at a place called Calvary, that He may never have to do it again.

Joy's Roommate

Optimism is joy's roommate.

Are you basically an optimistic person? Unfortunately, most people aren't. Monitor yourself in the following manner.

Begin to listen to yourself. Make yourself mindful of the remarkable number of negative responses or comments you make. When someone speaks to you, what is your response? When someone greets you with, "How are you?" do you respond, "Pretty good!"? Get that out of your vocabulary. Nothing is "pretty good." It is either good or not good. Listen to your automatic negative responses in normal conversation. Be attentive to your statements; monitor yourself.

Now ask yourself in all honesty, "Do I really believe myself?" Are you convinced that your automatic negative responses are true? Could a positive response just as well have been made? Could it be that you have just picked up on negative statements and are not aware of using them?

Next, practice new positive responses that are creative. Let them be "you" at your best. Think about the five basic greetings you get most often, and formulate how you are going to respond. You don't have to be cute or wise, just positive and joyous. Reflect on the five most common situations you are in, and plan your responses. After you have thought of them, practice saying them out loud a few times. Just saying them can make you feel better.

Make a mental note, or even better a written one, of the good things that happen to you in a day. Count your blessings. Most of us are good at counting. The problem is, we count the wrong things. We are adept at keeping a negative inventory. We count the red lights instead of the green ones. Make a note of even the small joys, pleasures, and blessings you have during the day. Reflect on them. Compute them on the screen of your mind. You will be amazed how good this makes you feel. Soon you will realize there are more good things in your life than you have been aware of.

Finally, start interpreting everything in the most positive light possible. View every person and event from this vantage point. Demand of yourself that you find the good or best meaning in all things. Soon you will amaze yourself. It may even seem you have moved into a new community. You might even find yourself thinking your luck has changed. A change of attitude can do that and more. Your stress will be reduced, pressure will abate, worries will dissipate, people will note your cheerfulness and your contagious happiness. Literally, a new you can emerge.

Joy can cross the street. It can come into your life.

Joy Is a Tool of Interpretation

Joy takes the salad of sorrow and garnishes it with gladness. "... Weeping may endure for a night, but joy cometh in the morning," said the Psalmist (Psalms 30:5). Even amid sorrow, we must realize we are en route to joy.

Joy gives *zest* to life. Zest is a vigorous and dynamic quality associated with joy. Joy generates this transferable, vivacious nature. Have you ever been around an expressive, joyous person? Didn't you feel energized? There is a depleted world begging us, "Energize me." What King David said to the Lord is applicable to friends; "... in thy presence is fulness of joy ... " (Psalms 16:11).

Joy keeps you at your *best*. There are things that dull joy, such as failure to do your best at an assignment. Excellence is activated by joy. There is no pressure to be the best, but there is a mandate to be *your* best. Being your best brings great pleasure—joy.

Joy helps you meet any *test*. A test is a challenge. Challenges are intended to give an occasion to demonstrate your character and capacity. Without joy, you have a cavity in your character. The apostle James said you should count it all joy when you have different tests. (*see* James 1:2). Joy awaits tests with happy expectation regarding the outcome.

Joy gives you *rest*. A parenthesis amid perplexity is needed. Joy allows it. Joy dispels the draining emotions of life. It is the sentry that guards the heart from pessimistic assailants. Joy takes the sting out of stress and dismantles tension.

Joy realizes you are *blessed*. Joy takes into account the good and the productive. It isn't being oblivious to problems and difficulties, it is simply putting them in their proper perspective and dramatizing the hidden blessings inherent in them. Joy doesn't stop there—it focuses on the positive and pleasant things. Whereas most people ignore them, the joyous person revels in them and recounts them.

Joy should be your life's *crest*. Gloom carries a can of spray paint in its hand, awaiting an opportunity to write paralyzing graffiti on the walls of your imagination. The crest of joy wards off any such attack. It shields the mind from infectious implications and poisonous precepts. Shine your shield. Make sure your joy shows. Wear your crest with zest because it is the best and will help you meet any test knowing you are blessed.

Resolving to let joy shine through you regardless of circumstances will not result in an utopian environment. Pictures will still hang crooked on the wall, dust bunnies will still gather under furniture, you will still get hangnails, and family members will often fail to cooperate. Amid all that, you can be an island of joy in the sea of despair. Provide a safe harbor for those who seek shelter in the cove of your compassion. Attitudes around you may remain negative, conditions may be trying and potentials ominous, but your attitude can overshadow them.

Joy is not intended for you at some point in the future—it is here and now. It is an attitude, a state of mind. Joy does not result from improved conditions and attitudes around you. If you are building and growing, your joy will increase.

One reason people do not have joy is that they are rushing through life to get to better times. By then, it is often too late. Slow down and open your eyes now.

Your attitude is the one thing no one else can control. It is at your exclusive control. Therefore, resolve: My attitude henceforth, regardless of circumstances, will be _____.

enJOY!

8

Know the Troubled Waters

Years ago, before navigation became sophisticated, a young man applied to be a pilot in the harbor of New Orleans. The port master interviewing him asked, "Do you know where all the shallow waters, sandbars, and rocky shoals are?"

"No sir," was the young man's reply.

"Well, how do you expect to be a pilot and guide ocean vessels safely to the dock if you don't know where they are?"

Instantly came the reply, "Sir, I know where they aren't, and that is where I would expect to guide the ships."

By knowing where potential problems are likely to be encountered, they can be avoided. Know the clear channels and stay in them.

Redbook magazine asked 730 marriage counselors to identify the most common problems that separate couples. The ten most common problems indicating troubled waters, in their order of frequency, were:

1. A breakdown in communication
2. The loss of shared goals or interests
3. Sexual incompatibility
4. Infidelity
5. The excitement and fun have gone out of marriage
6. Money
7. Conflicts about children
8. Alcohol and drug abuse
9. Women's equality issue
10. In-laws

Beth and Bob were a living clinic exhibiting all ten of these eroding elements. Few marriages have ever been besieged by more adverse factors.

Beth, a beautiful woman from a cultured background, was married to Bob, the successful son of an oil baron. Throughout college they were the "Ken and Barbie" on campus. Their achievements seemed to be an ongoing "Can you top this?"

Every asset desirable for a good marriage was theirs. Life had been good to them, as they walked the aisle to become Mr. and Mrs. Only a few years elapsed before the question was, "Whatever became of that lovely couple on the top of the wedding cake?"

These two, so magnetically attracted to each other, had multiple interests. They were intently interested in each other before marriage, but had no time to consider what elements were needed to make a bond in marriage. In marriage, their diverse interests emerged.

With a background of smooth sailing in a safe harbor, the turbulent open waters of marriage drove them toward shipwreck. They were so unsuspecting of troubled waters they never took time to see what they might encounter in marriage.

Having been chosen "Most Likely to Succeed" and "Miss Personality" in school, they were stunned when they realized they had lost touch with each other and could not communicate. Their spontaneity of talk imperceptibly slipped away. She would ask questions and he would interpret them as her being nosy. Her flippant responses to some of his remarks caused him to think of her as unreliable. Eventually she started chattering incessantly and monopolizing the conversation. He lost interest and tuned her out.

Impass!

Guidelines for safe passage through such a swelling sea follow. If you are where Beth and Bob were, consider these points carefully.

A Breakdown in Communication

Communications researcher Albert Mehrabian has explored the mystery of communication in an attempt to help persons achieve better success. He suggests that the following formula reveals the correlation between words and other factors in communication:

    7 percent—words alone
    38 percent—tone and inflection
    55 percent—facial expression, posture, and gestures

Words alone are not enough. When a breakdown in communications is noticed because of an absence of words, the situation is already in an advanced stage. Words are the last to go. Long before they do, a breakdown in the other areas of expression exists. We must monitor our full range of means of communication, making sure our words are not saying one thing and our tone and inflection another.

To keep your channels of communication open:

Recognize the human need to know Share your life totally with your partner. Answer every question warmly, realizing it expresses a desire to know.

Strive to be reliable Always be truthful. Avoid an "I had my fingers crossed" approach to communication. Reliability in speech builds confidence in a relationship.

Never monopolize the conversation Let there be a 50-50 split. When one partner utilizes more than the proper percentage of conversation, the other feels suppressed. When one partner utilizes more than 70 percent of conversation time, trouble is inevitable.

Be attentive There is power in a listening ear. Listening attentively suggests to the one speaking that you appreciate his or her importance and opinion. Pay attention. Remove barriers to good communication such as TV, newspapers, or other distractions. Give the speaker a sense of your involvement in what is being said.

Beth and Bob, who were once a single integrated unit, soon became two lonely, competing individuals.

Bob took on a mistress. No, not a sexy member of the opposite sex, but his work. He had the good fortune to have a superb job with superior income that was interesting and challenging. He found it very rewarding. His inherited tendency toward becoming a workaholic became dominant. In his work he could communicate and people were responsive. The worse conditions became at home, the more appreciation he had for a forum in which his word was heard.

Beth became a club bum. Her primary escape was tennis and a number of commendable community projects. Though both are good, either can become a sponge to absorb time and energy.

It was as though two who had traveled the same road for so long were now traveling in opposite directions on that road. Circumstances eventually drove them reluctantly to consider remedial steps toward a renewed marriage.

The Loss of Shared Goals or Interests

If two missiles fired from different positions are targets for the same mark, they are constantly coming closer to each other. When two lives are united in striving for a common goal, those lives are drawn closer together.

Unfortunately many couples never identify what their goals are, so they can work toward them as a team. It is wise to talk your goals out and discuss them fully. After doing so, it is practical to write them down and refine them.

Make sure that any goal decision is not unilateral. That is, be sure you are agreed and that the decision is bilateral—one on which both parties are agreed. It's a critical error to assume both of you are agreed on a goal without verifying it through discussion.

Work at developing common interests. This might take some compromise and adjustment. When interests vary greatly, people can be pulled apart, growing in different areas. This fact even applies to spiritual growth. There needs to be parallel growth.

Some interests will naturally differ; however, there must be some major interests that can be developed together. Let this be a process of development. Enter into your partner's interests. Be open and expectant as to what interests your mate. Explore things that can be done together.

Sexual Incompatibility

Just a few years earlier, Beth had been the sex symbol on campus and Bob the virile athlete. The chemistry was too good not to work. Their inordinate expectations relating to sex in marriage placed them at a disadvantage. Their expectations were so high that even the most sexually compatible couple would have been disappointed. Their only understanding of sex related to biological self-fulfillment. Such an approach always results in emptiness.

Sex is the great American hoax. It gets such exaggerated

Know the Troubled Waters

play that it is impossible to live up to its mythological reputation. People who use eggs for golf balls play short games. People who try to use sex as a panacea for all problems are destined to disappointment. Excessive expectation leads to frustration.

Plastic sex devalues and dehumanizes a person. Sex is more than biological fulfillment. When it becomes only that for either partner, it loses its meaning for the other. When sex is reduced to a mere animal expression, it is void of its greatest fulfillment. There can be love without sex, but there should never be sex without love. It should always be a by-product of love. Not every expression of love should be interpreted as leading to sexual activity. However, there should never be sexual activity that is not preceded by and involving love.

It's estimated that less than 2 percent of sexual incompatibility is physical. Since sexual incompatibility is such a prominent contributor to marriage problems, the other 98 percent of the cause needs to be identified. It has been—it's a mental attitude. There must be a loving spirit that is demonstrated in unsexually related ways for sex to be mutually gratifying. Sex is not intended to be a mere union. It is rather designed to be communion.

Many mistakenly look to sex to correct all of their problems. Actually all their problems complicate their sexual expression and result in it being blamed and spoken of as being incompatible.

"Bob doesn't seem to understand me or have time for me anymore," said Beth wistfully. The new male friend she was dining with at the club responded attentively and reassuringly. A simple beginning of a slide into an unfulfilling, guilt-ridden pit of passion was begun with that statement.

Bob had his audience, also. His starved male ego reached out for reassurance of his masculinity. More than one insecure young beauty was responsive.

Bob and Beth were both amazed by the ease with which they found sexual partners outside their marriage. They found this biologically satisfying and ego fulfilling, but also character depleting. The trade-off wasn't worth it. Guilt and self-dissatisfaction resulted.

Infidelity

Sexual fidelity is the most unpopular of all virtues. Infidelity is directly and indirectly encouraged by all forms of secular media. It is the "in thing." The fields of entertainment, advertising, and news are saturated with it.

I have seen much pain and grief caused by infidelity, but I have never heard of anyone being destroyed by fidelity.

Many people quickly point to infidelity as the primary biblical ground for divorce. Though divorce for infidelity is allowable, this allowance is at no time given as an encouragement to divorce. Even infidelity, as grievous a sin as it is and as injurious as it is, can be forgiven. Healing can occur.

Infidelity suggests a chicken-or-egg situation. Does infidelity cause problems in a marriage, or do problems in a marriage cause infidelity? It varies in different relationships. There is no doubt that infidelity complicates all other problems and makes them more acute.

Infidelity is fool's gold, which has the appearance of gold but not its value. Promiscuity has the promise of fidelity, but not the reality. It is the most ignominious of injuries. It defrauds, debases, devaluates, and denies one's mate of a sense of worth.

Any marriage partner who decides to be unfaithful can be so within one hour. It is not difficult to be unfaithful. It takes character, willpower, and love to remain faithful.

Even if this holocaust occurs in your marriage, it can and should be overcome. It can result in a better marriage.

The Excitement and Fun Have Gone out of Marriage

"You are no fun to live with," shouted Beth.
"Neither are you," echoed Bob.
Both were right. They had failed to ask themselves, "Am I

fun to live with?" Each knew the other wasn't fun—they had done so much living apart from each other that their marriage had been drained of all pleasure. Both were good role players for so long a time that their friends had no idea they were play acting. It was all show and no substance. The frame remained, but the function was gone. Their inherent fun-loving natures drove them to look for other sources of pleasure, always looking somewhere other than to each other. They consistently looked outside the home and apart from the marriage, hopelessly failing to find fulfillment.

Most likely, the fun has actually gone from all phases of life if it is gone from marriage. Unfortunately some enticement often comes along outside of marriage that promises excitement and fun. This untimely lure can cause infidelity.

Candidly: Are you fun to live with?

Resolve that henceforth you are going to be fun to live with. Think of what you have done to rob your relationship of its intended joy. What can you do to revitalize it? Work on your sense of humor, personality, and spirit of adventure.

If you aren't fun to live with, a new mate wouldn't do you any good; you would simply spoil another person's good time. Start where you are, with those who comprise your extended family, and determine to contribute to their excitement and fun. Life is more than this, but it must have these elemental ingredients to remain fresh.

Review old recreational and entertainment activities. If they are still possible, try them again. They once brought pleasure and might well do so again. Many new and creative means of recreation and entertainment are available. Explore interests, be innovative. Initiate new projects that will bring delight. Even if your partner does not respond positively at first, you will be setting a mood by example.

Church is an ideal place to meet new friends and establish a wholesome social base, as well as strengthen your faith. Many churches are mindful of family needs and provide for them. Such a church is a good hub around which the family can orbit.

Money

Mismanagement of finances will drain the most abundant bank account. It didn't for Beth and Bob, but misconceptions regarding money became a tension point in the marriage.

Bob accused Beth of driving him to overachieve so she could overspend. Beth criticized Bob for slinging money around like glue—she thought he was stingy. He considered himself frugal. Eruptions over money became more frequent, while she sought ways of secretly spending it and he hunted for ways to reduce her access to it.

Their attitude regarding money and their failure to plan its use was the problem. Under those circumstances, no amount of money is sufficient. That which is often looked upon as being a panacea for happiness robbed them of it.

There are basics concerning money that every couple must apply.

The amount of money you have is of little importance. Your attitude toward it is fundamental to your happiness. The love of money is indeed the root of all evil.

Talk about money. Many couples get into trouble because they don't talk about it. Some feel they have so much they don't need to discuss it. Others are embarrassed because they have so little that they don't discuss it. In both instances, the same result often follows; they spend themselves into trouble. When both parties fully understand the financial picture, there can be mutual cooperation in living within the means. To do this, there is a simple formula:

> When your outgo
> Exceeds your income
> Then your upkeep
> Becomes your downfall.
> Live within your means.

Have a joint checking account, with one of you keeping a simple but accurate accounting. Establish a time each month when you talk over your financial picture.

Develop a budget. Let it be a guideline, not a straitjacket.

Make it realistic, conforming to your income. Make all major decisions regarding primary expenditures and investments together. The one who understands finances better should patiently instruct the other, so you will learn together.

Make an inventory of all household items. It's a good idea to photograph all of the items in your possession and keep the prints someplace outside your house, in the event of fire or a burglary.

Make a will, regardless of your age. Review it periodically and revise it as needed. Don't delay another day in doing this.

Conflicts About Children

Even from the beginning of Bob and Beth's marriage, children had caused a conflict. First, he wanted them sooner than she did. Finally, when they became parents of two delightful children, the children became pawns in their parents' quest for acceptance. At one stage, it was a race to see who could out-parent the other. Later, as their relationship as husband and wife deteriorated, their roles as Dad and Mother were effectively forfeited. Neither would discipline a child, for fear of losing the child's attachment. As they lost control over the children, they also lost their children's respect.

Two perfectly beautiful children, born to wealthy parents, became heathens in high fashion. Victims of neglect, they sought attention through disobedience.

Fortunately the marriage was helped from outside by a church youth group that warmly took in the adolescents. In a loving environment with peers of strong character, the children soon developed strong moral and spiritual values of their own. Eventually this was the initial factor in salvaging the home.

Before this aspect of your family fails, consider the following. Children are artists at dividing parents in order to get their own way. They can play parents against each other like a cymbal player. A united front is essential for both the children and the marriage.

Parents should confer with each other in the absence of the

children in order to decide how they will handle certain situations. Even if the parents disagree over a certain point, they should wait until alone to work it out. Never quarrel about a child-related decision in the presence of the child. If a mistake is made, wait until a later opportunity to talk it out and resolve it. Seeing your togetherness gives the children confidence and assurance.

In relating to your children, try these techniques:

1. Be attentive to what your children say. Be a good listener.
2. Ask your children's opinions about things in which their insight will be helpful. Give each child a sense of "I count."
3. Compliment your children on acts of self-discipline, courtesy, helpfulness, creativity, and industriousness.
4. Note and commend your children's improvement, regardless of how small. Build a sense of self-worth.
5. Pray together for your children in their presence. Children need to grow up with certain family traditions fixed in their minds, which gives them something to relate to and from which to draw strength.
6. Let there be no doubt in your children that you as parents love each other and them. Never let them feel that there might be a fracture in your relationship. This heightens their insecurity and results in adverse behavior.
7. A matchless way in which to teach your children to respect authority is for you to be subject to the authority of God in your life. Children learn by observation.

Alcohol and Drug Abuse

Alcohol was Bob's great escape. Cocaine was Beth's path to bliss. Both were rapidly reduced to near zombies before each saw himself mirrored in the other. Fear of what was happening drove them to seek help. A long, painful road back caused them to have such contempt for their enslaving masters as never to use them again. They remain a dry alcoholic and a cured junkie.

Today's youth are well informed in the area of pharmacology. They know drugs and their physical and psychological impact. Yet youthful drug abuse abounds. Why? One principal reason is parental example. Children see little difference between consuming alcohol and smoking marijuana. To them it's like arguing which is worse, leprosy or cancer. Neither has much to commend it.

Children know the health hazards involved in smoking and overeating. When a parent does any of these, the child learns to excuse himself for similar conduct. As a result, over 5,000 families annually go through the grief of burying a teenager because of an accident involving alcohol.

A chemical curtain is gossamer. You can't hide behind it; reality will still be waiting when the curtain is drawn. Escaping through drugs is running into a disastrous mine field more deadly than the most adverse of circumstances.

Alcohol and many other drugs are addictive. Even those that do not addict may cause a person to become psychologically dependent. No one has ever set out by design to be an alcoholic or addict. The chemical controls the body physiologically. Willpower is often not adequate to free the subject from this brutal master.

Since addiction is not predictable, abstinence is the only sure way to avoid it. I have seen much misery, grief, and poverty caused by alcohol and drugs, but I have never known of one person who suffered from abstinence.

Women's Equality Issues

In the case of Beth and Bob, two people who had once been mutually supportive and responsive drifted apart. Partly because of forfeiture of roles and partially because of some philosophies shared around the club, Beth became dominant in their relationship. The more assertive she became, the more acquiescent Bob was. Initial heated arguments were replaced with passiveness and smoldering resentment. Beth's facade hid her growing insecurity. Her uncertainty in defying her instincts made her tense and irritable. Bob, being threatened, retreated further into his business, where his authoritative role could find expression. Their drift apart was slow but certain.

Roles must be understood in order for fulfillment to exist.

Equality really isn't the issue—misunderstanding regarding it is the serious problem. Neither masculine suppression nor feminine assertiveness is the answer. Scripture calls both men and women to mutual submission and active discipleship. Their compatible and cooperative roles, as defined in the Bible, offer the only basis for avoiding the battle of the sexes.

Christian men should take a closer look at personal biases and feelings. Are they biblical or traditional? Do you feel a need to be superior? If so, why? Is yours a Christlike attitude?

Christian women should evaluate how they can demonstrate their God-given gifts. Do you feel a need to be more aggressive and demanding? If so, why? Is yours a Christlike attitude?

Husbands and wives must live by the standard set in Ephesians 5:21, "Submitting yourselves one to another in the fear of God."

Submission is above and superior to obedience. Obedience could be coercion to outward conformity. Submission is leaning upon, trusting in, and even abandoning one's rights, energies, and desires to an object of trust. Stubbornness and rebellion are foreign in nature to submission. Submission is simple and complete faith in the providence of God and His earthly authority. It is confidence and trust in the person we love.

Male and female, God created us as equals. For husbands and wives, He lovingly defined our different roles. Neither role is superior to the other. They are intended to fulfill and complete each other.

In-laws

Loving parents from stable homes were not unobservant of what was happening to the marriage of Bob and Beth. Instinctively, both families wanted to help. Living in relatively close proximity to both families made Bob and Beth resentful of the efforts of the other's parents.

Only maturity and a good Bible orientation by both sets of parents prevented disaster in this area. They conversed together, working out a plan of nonintervention and mutual support. Thus they took the pressure off at this critical point.

Reflect on these principles regarding a potential sandbar that will ground any marriage.

When there were only two people on earth, Adam and Eve, God in His wisdom foresaw that in-law problems would arise in the future. As a preventative, He prescribed that a man leave his father and mother for the sake of marriage. Whether this leaving is physical or not, it must be psychological. The in-laws must let go, and the offspring must go. Trouble is inevitable if this is not done. No two couples are always going to approach every situation exactly alike. Sooner or later, a difference of opinion will arise. When it does, the offspring instinctively will be expected to subordinate all opinions to those of the parent, which is not wise or right.

Make it a point to cultivate your in-laws. Remember their anniversaries, birthdays, and holidays with cards or gifts. A note now and then can help accent good relationships.

Never attack the reputation of your in-laws in front of your mate. It will be taken personally. Instinctively, lifelong defense devices will be brought into play. This becomes divisive. If there is a conflict, deal with principles and not personalities. Make it clear that it is an *issue* over which you disagree, and not an *individual*.

To love your in-laws is to love your mate. To love your mate is to love yourself.

Any one of the problems mentioned in this chapter, or a combination of any of them, can cause problems in the best of marriages. Don't feel you are immune. If your marriage is suffering from any of them, you have no reason to feel like the Lone Ranger.

Make a mental note of them and plan to avoid them if possible. If it isn't possible to avoid them, be advised that your marriage can survive any and all of them. Don't let them defeat you.

Oh, yes—Bob and Beth. They are Exhibit A of a couple that sailed all the troubled waters with success. Their Christian heritage, a lifelong success orientation that motivated them to resolve all the issues, and competent, prolonged counsel has given them a stable home once again.

Their message to others is simple. Avoidance is better than painful and costly steps to recovery. Also, there is more self-fulfillment in making any required effort to restore a marriage than in quitting too easily.

Take heart. Their marriage is now a functioning and fulfilling one. Yours can be, also. Now that you know the troubled waters, plot your course to sail in safe seas.

9

Traits of a Good Relationship

It was a lovely spring day when Dot phoned Carl to tell him she wasn't feeling well. The tone of her voice said, "Please hurry home!" Every light seemed to be red and traffic slower than ever as he raced home. As he rushed in, it was immediately apparent Dot had lost her orientation.

Without delay he quickly sped her to the hospital. Dot being a nurse, she was well beloved by the medical staff; as professionals and friends they worked cautiously to save her life. A sigh of relief by the lead doctor indicated that her vital signs had stabilized. Patiently the family began their long love vigil. Every report from the doctors increased tensions. Then the sad news came: Dot had suffered severe brain damage as a result of the stroke. Her future was uncertain at best.

Days dragged into weeks as Dot slipped deeper into a coma. The hospital could do no more for her. She was taken home, and weeks turned into months. For nearly thirty-six months, the family and professionals cared for her. They were a living epistle of divine love. They did for her what she could not do for herself. Compassionate concern was showered upon her consistently. Verbal expressions of love were shared in the hope that she was able to comprehend, even if she could not respond. Holidays and anniversaries were celebrated in her presence in the event she could understand. TLC (tender loving care) typified her family support system.

Theirs was a divine type of love, in that they gave without response. Our heavenly Father gives to us, and we often fail to respond. As that does not keep Him from doing and providing for us, so Dot's unresponsiveness did not dampen her family's efforts. Whereas she could not say thank you, we often *will* not say it to our divine benefactor. They mirrored the mind of the Father in their actions. They demonstrated a classic example of true love for all their friends.

Ultimately, the end came suddenly. Its arrival was a long and arduous march through an agonizing arena. Dot died the object of Carl's fully expressed love.

Years before, the two had become one when they pledged to be true to each other for better or for worse. No one dreamed on that delightful wedding day that the worse could involve such anguish. When the end came, the vow had been fulfilled.

How could Carl and his family endure such a prolonged ordeal? Simply because they had forged a good relationship in better times as well as the previous worse times. Because of the relation, the ship wasn't scuttled in stormy waters.

A good relationship is like life insurance: If you need it and you haven't got it, it's too late to get it. Its development should be a lifelong ambition.

A seed of significance in a good relationship is friendship. As it grows, its roots permeate all of life. A friend is a person with whom your soul can go naked. You don't need to put on anything around a friend. You don't have to be better or worse, just yourself. When you are with a friend, you feel like a person who has just been declared innocent. It isn't necessary to be on perpetual guard. A friend is like a fire that purges all you do, like water that cleanses what you say, like a hot beverage that warms you to the bone. Friends understand. You can achieve with a friend or fail with him, laugh or weep with him. A friend sees, knows, and loves you. Such understanding is foundational to a good relationship.

A marriage based on such friendship is not just for better or worse, but for good.

Marriage is no fairyland where people live happily ever after. For some the wedding ring isn't a symbol of love but an arena for fights. A resolute determination to build a good, growing relationship must exist.

The apostle Peter shared insights into how husbands and wives should relate. He concluded his insights on the subject by relating traits of a good relationship. Though this passage deals with interpersonal relationships in general, it applies to husbands and wives as well as the total family. Five traits are noted: "Finally, be ye all of one mind, having compassion one of another, love as brethren, be pitiful, be courteous" (1 Peter 3:8).

Harmony

For there to be harmony in music, there must be a chord. For there to be harmony in marriage, there must be accord. Peter exhorts people to be of one mind. Most couples agree on that but disagree on *which* mind. We must be like a great orchestra, where each instrument differs from the other but all are tuned to one standard. Most musical instruments are tuned to a standard 440 vibrations per second. The proper standard for a harmonious marriage must be Jesus Christ. He is the "A-440" of the husband/wife relationship.

Life in tune with Him results in harmony, becoming a beautiful adventure.

Marriage, an institution divinely established, becomes a holy trust from the Lord. Living in close proximity with anyone will result in frequent conflicts and occasional heartaches. Only a good, growing relationship can survive. One not according to God's plan can't be a good one.

Second Corinthians 6:14 gives a framework for such relationships: "Be ye not unequally yoked together with unbelievers: for what fellowship hath righteousness with unrighteousness? and what communion hath light with darkness?"

Fellowship, an important ingredient in any relationship, becomes more difficult when two do not agree on a spiritual plane. Fundamental differences exist between persons who do not share a mutually expressive personal faith. Two who do not share such a common conviction have disagreed on the principal basis of any agreement.

In speaking of the marriage of widows, 1 Corinthians 7:39 says, "The wife is bound by the law as long as her husband liveth; but if her husband be dead, she is at liberty to be married to whom she will; only in the Lord." If a widow is free to marry only in the Lord, logic suggests no believer is free to wed outside of the Lord, that is, to a nonbeliever.

When emotions short-circuit intellect, disaster can result. Solomon, a man blessed with the divine gift of wisdom, sinned at this critical point. "Solomon brought up the daughter of Pharaoh out of the city of David unto the house that he had built for her: for he said, My wife shall not dwell in the house of David king of Israel, because the places are holy, whereunto the ark of the Lord hath come" (2 Chronicles 8:11). He married a woman who was of such character as not to desire or deserve to come into the house of God. Solomon, the wisest man ever to live, let his heart run ahead of his head. The uneven yoke favored his wife, of whom it is said, "his wives turned away his heart after other gods" (1 Kings 11:4).

Years later, when the remnant of Israel returned under the leadership of Nehemiah, they began to intermarry with unbelievers. Solomon was used by Nehemiah as an example of the fearful end of those who disobey God and marry against His will. They had no harmony, thus discord filled their palatial quarters.

For a relationship to be harmonious, the parties need to have everything possible in common. Harmony is not only needed on the spiritual plane but in such areas as culture, education, social, economic, and family backgrounds. Commonality avoids chasms that have to be bridged. Folly alone would allow a person to ignore differences that divide and think emotion will overcome it all. Such fissures can be too taxing on a potentially good marriage.

Numerous advantages result from a couple progressing together. If one outgrows the other in any area of life, a gap widens between them. Open conversation about progress in all areas of a relationship helps. Encouragement comes from keeping pace and growing together. Growth together in all the areas noted produces intimacy.

For harmony to prevail, instruments must play together. Couples should do things together that give a mutual opportunity of expression. By doing only competitive things together, couples tend to become combatants, not colleagues. Such activities divide rather than unite. Oneness must exist on all levels. In this way a delight in those things that blend our efforts develops. Try these activities together:

1. Share work projects
2. Enjoy common recreation
3. Worship together
4. Develop mutual hobbies
5. Create collective self-improvement activities

If an activity doesn't unite you, it isn't worth doing together. No one's success or pleasure should be at the expense of the other.

Dot and Carl had built their lives around their children

and their activities. It is little wonder that in their great hour of need, the children rallied around them. Having received their parents' support in their youth, the children responded to their needs. Faithfulness fostered faithfulness. A lifelong example of a controlled temperament provided the strings on which their victory in agony was orchestrated.

Heartfelt

A second trait of a good relationship cited by Peter is found in having compassion one for another. The heart of the translation is found in the Greek word *sumpathes* used by the apostle. It denotes suffering with another, to be affected similarly, to share distress through the circumstances of another person. This mental attitude has visceral validity.

A good marriage has feeling. We are to sorrow with those who sorrow and rejoice with those who rejoice. To fail to do so is to fail to share fully in another's experience.

Paul and Pippy had a young love. It was expressed vigorously physically. They had not been married long when things began to change. The ardor cooled. Expression waned. He knew things were not as good as they once were, but was stunned when she told him she had filed for divorce. The unexpected suddenness of the announcement was followed by immediate expression of deep bitterness. Her "I don't love you" outburst shocked him.

In a daze, he pleaded for an explanation. Finally, after reality set in, he asked her when she stopped loving him. She replied, "Do you remember about three months after we were married, when I called to tell you I had been involved in an accident?" He acknowledged remembering the incident. Pippy continued, "When I told you, your response was, 'How badly is the car damaged?' I knew you were crazy about the car, but when you didn't bother to ask if I was hurt, I was truly hurt. That is when I started to stop loving you."

He had missed his moment to share in her suffering.

Traits of a Good Relationship

Though she fortunately was not injured physically, she was deeply involved in the trauma of the accident. He completely failed to relate to her at a time and in a way that could naturally have drawn them closer to each other. Failure to do so fractured their relationship. He failed to participate actively in the fellowship of her suffering. This failure indicated they were not feeling together. This was the first symptom of their not really being together in a heartfelt way.

To have a heartfelt relationship, a person must strive to understand the emotional makeup of another. It shows a sense of caring and evidences concern. It is an admirable indirect way of saying, "I love you." Attentiveness is a symptom of love.

Failure to be attentive has resulted in many great moments being overlooked and many people ignored.

On a cool, windy, autumn day in 1910, the director of the renowned Parisian Folies-Bergère was approached by a young would-be songwriter. Inattentively, the great maestro hurriedly scanned the score. Disdainfully shaking his head he said, "I am sorry, but I would have no use for this, son. I don't want to sound discouraging, but to tell you the truth, I'm afraid you won't find anyone who will be interested in your 'Alexander's Ragtime Band,' Mr. Berlin." In the days before the inflated dollar, Irving Berlin made over a quarter of a million dollars on that song. It cost the uninvolved director even more dearly.

Similar failure to relate in a heartfelt way has cost many a marriage partner dearly. Insensitivity to opportunities to relate to your beloved through an event of importance weakens a marriage. By capitalizing on highs and lows, we can establish a closer relationship.

Valuing another's opinion shows heartfelt concern. Involvement is shown by asking such questions as: "What do you think of that?"; "How do you feel about it?"; "Please share your opinion on this."

When you ask—listen!

Your follow-up will indicate how deeply you are involved

with the person answering. A person should always have the confidence of knowing his or her opinion counts and that the attitude is important to you. This gives a sense of worth. The fact that a person feels he counts with you is vital. It indicates that a good relationship exists.

Christ, our example, is often represented as being moved by compassion. He is depicted as feeling right along with the people to whom He was relating. His relationship with Lazarus, Mary, and Martha is revealed in the short text which states "Jesus wept." The word translated *wept* meant He shook with convulsive sorrow. The crowd, seeing this, spoke of how He loved Lazarus. Christ's relationship with the family was heartfelt. To the crowd, it revealed love.

A heartfelt relationship will:

1. Make you mindful of a "we" and "our" outlook, not an "I" or "mine" attitude.
2. Free you from oversensitivity by making you empathetic with others and less mindful of yourself.
3. Motivate fair play. This incorporates consideration for others under all conditions.
4. Curb your temper so that you will in no way and with no word injure your partner.
5. Enable patience to be manifest at all times.
6. Cultivate a pleasant disposition in order not to offend in word or deed.
7. Prevent an effort to dominate and result in a willingness to compromise.

Happy

In 1 Peter 3:8, Peter identified another trait of a good relationship by the expression "love as brethren." Such love produces happiness.

Not to love a brother is unnatural. Brotherly love supersedes all differences. Jonathan and David are examples of such love. By birthright, Jonathan was to inherit the

Traits of a Good Relationship

throne—he was entitled to it. However, he clearly understood that it was the will of God for David to ascend to the throne. His love for David prompted Jonathan to rejoice over David's emerging eminence at his own expense. That is love. Ambitious aspirants to the throne had killed for it. Brotherly love caused acquiescence to the advantage of another one who was loved. Where this kind of love prevails, a lasting relationship exists. Uncompetitive rejoicing with each other's successes builds a bond. Sharing equally in others' sorrows does the same.

Phileo is one of the three Greek words for love. It refers to affection or concern for another human being. It does not occur in the Bible with regard to marriage. Nowhere in the New Testament does the word meaning strong feeling or passion (*eros*) appear. *Agape* love, such as Christ had for His Church, is the type a husband is to have for his wife. This word for love speaks of a volitional, unconditional love, the depth of which is measured by sacrifice.

Feelings are a by-product, and those feelings might well result in erotic love. If so, in proper context of husband and wife, that is a bonus. Husbands are not told to feel warmly or kindly toward their wives. That is a consequence of truly loving her. *Agape* love is not comprised of what one feels, but consists of what one *does*.

There are some conditions in married life where the relationship doesn't have a chance if the two are not the best of friends who love as brothers. Sometimes the world boxes you in so tightly that you have no other friend to which to turn.

Again Christ emerges as our peerless example. He said, "A new commandment I give unto you, That ye love one another; as I have loved you, that ye also love one another" (John 13:34).

He dramatically demonstrated His love for us by giving Himself for us. With Him as our example, we are constantly to be giving ourselves for one another. Observe these conditions:

1. Don't be selfish with your time
2. Don't be greedy with your willingness to serve
3. Don't be small in your thoughtfulness
4. Try giving yourself away

The gratifying spin-off is happiness.

If you love God, you are willing to love as brothers. This is one more reason why it is imperative for partners in marriage to be of a mutual faith. When one doesn't love God, a basic lack of understanding of love exists. It is written, "If a man say, I love God, and hateth his brother, he is a liar: for he that loveth not his brother whom he hath seen, how can he love God whom he hath not seen?"(1 John 4:20).

The stronger your love is for God, the richer it is for your brother. In order to grow in your ability to love as brethren, grow in your devotion to God. To show your love for God demonstrates your love for your brethren (mate).

Hearty

Peter used the Greek word *eusplachnoi* to note the next noble characteristic of a good relationship. It comes from the root word which means "be pitiful." It means to be goodhearted.

This was written before medical science progressed to its present point of sophistication and comprehension. During the time of this writing, it was believed that thoughts were carried in the blood. They became conscious thoughts when the blood coursed through the brain. It was also known that the heart pumped the blood and sent it on its course. The heart being the point of circulation's origin, it was thought to be the place of all thoughts' origination. Thus, when the heart is the reference, it relates to one's basic mind set. Hence, the appeal is for all basic thoughts to be of a tender and compassionate nature. A person who was tenderhearted was one whose every thought was gentle.

Historically, the expression had an even deeper meaning.

It was used to speak of the essence of God. God was considered tenderhearted in essence, which marked Him as distinct from all pagan gods. They were envisioned as vindictive and harsh. Contrast is shown between the true God and false gods. A similar contrast exists between a person who strives to be pitiful and an ungodlike person.

A gem worthy of your mind reads: "And whatsoever ye do, do it heartily, as to the Lord, and not unto men" (Colossians 3:23).

In order to maintain a good relationship, supernatural motivation is often needed. Sometimes your partner may so injure or alienate you that you find it difficult to respond properly. At this point, envision the partner as Christ's proxy. Consider what you are doing as being done unto Him. You are in effect doing to and/or for your partner what you would do for Christ, were He in your partner's position. Surely you would relate to Christ heartily. This enables one to maintain enthusiasm in a relationship.

If you do what you do to garner Christ's approval, you will do it with enthusiasm. He, as the source of enthusiasm, will enable you to so respond. The Greek root words used in combination to form the word *enthusiasm* reveal this. *En* means within. *Theos* means God. Originally enthusiasm meant "God within you." Christ as the fountainhead of every thought will motivate a person. Such a heart belongs to an enthusiastic person. With Him—your tenderhearted God—at the point of origin of all your attitudes, you will "be pitiful," that is, inclined to tenderheartedness. A good relationship feeds off such a spirit.

Emotions rise and fall like the tide. Partners in marriage must be observant of each other's mood swings. If one is down, the other should resolve to try to pick that one up, knowing that he or she will likely at some point be the one down. In life, Dot was a buoyant person. There had been many times she picked up the spirits of her entire family. Certainly Carl had been lifted by her radiance and optimism many times in their years together. Though it was never said, he doubtless was inspired during her long incapacitation by memories of her loyalty in having lifted him.

Humble

Peter notes an indispensable trait of a good relationship when he advises, "be courteous." *Philophron* is the Greek word. It means friendly thoughtfulness. Humility is one facet of the word's meaning, kindness another.

Humility is one of those things that just when you think you have it, you have lost it. "Wherefore let him that thinketh he standeth take heed lest he fall" (1 Corinthians 10:12).

Humility does not require having a lower opinion of yourself than of others, nor does it mean having a devalued concept of your gifts. It is simply the blessed freedom from thinking about yourself at all. The sick idea of having to think constantly of yourself as less worthy than others is false humility. It offers an inordinate preoccupation with yourself. Humility is having optimum consideration for others. It is getting yourself off your mind and your mind off yourself. A humble person is one who looks out for the welfare of others.

True humility is not an abject, groveling, self-devaluating spirit; it is simply a right estimate of ourselves and others as God sees us.

A spirit of superiority indicates that wrong comparisons are being made. A mountain shames a molehill until they are both humbled by the stars. When we begin to feel superior to someone, we have failed to look at our intended model—Christ.

Thomas à Kempis shared a truth that helps our outlook: "Do not consider yourself to have made any spiritual progress, unless you account yourself the least of all men. God walks with the humble; he reveals himself to the lowly; he gives understanding to the little ones; he discloses his meaning to pure minds, but hides his grace from the curious and proud."

It is hard to admit we have spoken without thinking, that

we have talked nonsense. How often we say things in haste and heat, without proper understanding or full meaning, and yet, because we have said it, stick to it and try to defend it as though it were right. How much wiser and more admirable it is to show the grace to detect and acknowledge a mistake. It gives others the assurance that we are learning, growing, improving, and developing, so the future will be better than the past.

A person who resolves to be courteous—that is, humble—will be thoughtful. You can show courtesy and humility by:

1. Marking and acknowledging important dates
2. Noting significant occasions
3. Never letting a special event pass
4. Expressing appreciation
5. Acknowledging thanks
6. Complimenting achievements
7. Building another's self-esteem

Have you ever known a thoughtful person you didn't admire? Probably not. Therefore, if you would like to be admired, be thoughtful. Don't do it simply to be admired—in doing it, you *will* be admired. By showing appreciation for others, you will be appreciated. This is twice good for a relationship.

Kindness is a becoming part of being courteous. Don't you enjoy being around kind people? If you are kind, people will enjoy being around you. Kindness draws like a magnet. Remember how good you felt the last time you showed kindness to a person? Kindness is a two-headed arrow. In blessing, you are blessed.

Wisely, in speaking of a virtuous woman, Solomon included something that is also true of a man, "... in her tongue is the law of kindness" (Proverbs 31:26). An ancient Hebrew saying is well-remembered: "Kindness is the beginning and the end of the law."

Rudeness repels. No one was ever helped by sarcasm—crushed, perhaps, if the sarcasm was clever enough, but never drawn nearer to the user—never. If you think sophisticated sarcasm is cute, forget it. Even if you enjoy it, don't plan on anyone else liking it. Conversely, kind words are heaven's music heard on earth. They exert power that seems to be beyond the norm; they influence as though they were the angels' song. It seems they can do what only God can do—soften the hard heart and cool the hot head.

We have yet to learn how to fully use kindness. A tender touch, an affectionate look, some kind act all speak of love as clearly as words. If you want to develop a good relationship, develop the art of being kind.

The sudden and dramatic way in which the relationship of Carl and Dot ended was the final flower in a garden long and well tended. No new traits emerged in the hour of their great emergency. Life had well rehearsed them for the moment when applied love would carry one without the reciprocal aid of the other. At social events, athletic contests, worship services, political rallies, and work at home, they had practiced these traits of a good relationship.

A memory bank of admiration, affection, and accord paid big dividends when heavily taxed. A bonus comes from knowing love lasts to the last.

When death came, it was easier to let Dot's hand go knowing death is the end—the *front* end of glory. Death is not the master of the house; it is only the servant of the King's house, appointed to open the gate and let the guests of the King enter into His eternal paradise.

"The Lord giveth and the Lord taketh away...." He always gives more than He takes. Remaining for Carl was the refreshing memory of a good relationship. For peace of mind, we should all live so as to have that consolation in death.

10

Tenderness and 24 Other Ways to Make a Marriage Work

Joanne had muscular dystrophy. Her physical disability resulted in her being confined to a wheelchair. Milt, her husband, was legally blind. His dark world was as limited as her chair-bound one was restrictive. Don't feel sorry for them—they had a beautiful relationship. This can be understood in light of Milt's explanation: "She is my eyes, and I am her legs."

Eyes and legs were just symbols of the total self for Milt and Joanne. They had become one. They embodied the adage, "What is thine is mine, and what is mine is thine."

First, they gave themselves to each other for better or worse. This happened long before she needed his legs and he needed her eyes. The commitment having been made, the vow was easy to keep.

Every couple has the equivalent of lost limbs and sight. It is a shame these shortcomings are not recognized as opportunities to become mutually interdependent. Unfortunately most couples interpret their limitations, restrictions, and handicaps as liabilities, when in reality they could draw them closer.

There were certain traits woven in the relationship of Joanne and Milt that were just as distinguishable as an accent thread woven into fine tapestry. Certain of these are recorded in Romans 12:9–21. They relate broadly to the total Christian community but have specific application to husbands and wives. Whether applied to the cosmic conflict or a couple's clash, they are valid.

The writer of Romans lists these in staccato fashion. Bronze these words and put them on the mantle of your mind. Reflect on them frequently in order to be able to make instant application.

> Let love be without dissimulation. Abhor that which is evil; cleave to that which is good. Be kindly affectioned one to another with brotherly love; in honour preferring one another; Not slothful in business; fervent in spirit; serving the Lord; Rejoicing in hope; patient in tribulation; continuing instant in prayer; Distributing to the necessity of saints; given to hospitality. Bless them which persecute you: bless, and curse not. Rejoice with them that do rejoice, and weep with them that weep. Be of the same mind one toward another. Mind not high things, but condescend to men of low estate. Be not wise in your own conceits. Recompense to no man evil for evil. Provide things honest in the sight of all men. If it be possible, as much as lieth in you, live peaceably with all men. Dearly beloved, avenge not yourselves, but

rather give place unto wrath: for it is written, Vengeance is mine; I will repay, saith the Lord. Therefore if thine enemy hunger, feed him; if he thirst, give him drink: for in so doing thou shalt heap coals of fire on his head. Be not overcome of evil, but overcome evil with good.

Romans 12:9–21

Tenderness

As a fine lock opens only with the right key, so this passage opens with the key to any good relationship, love. The Greek word employed is *agape*. It is a reference to absolute loyalty to its object. Heaven's larger-than-life example of this type love is the love Jesus Christ has for you. His life was a dynamic demonstration of *agape*.

Solomon spoke of the durability of love in a refreshing manner: "Many waters cannot quench love, neither can the floods drown it . . ." (Song of Solomon 8:7). True love, *agape*, is a fire fueled by an inextinguishable combustible. It is far more than mere emotions and of greater substance than simple sensation. It is love with a second wind—it goes on long after youthful passions have faded, allowing you to expose your inner being to your beloved. This exposure is not external, but internal.

The seasoned psychologist Rollo May speaks of the difficulty many people have in this regard: "It is strange that in our society the things that go into our relationship—the sharing of tastes, fantasies, dreams, hopes and fears—seem to make people more shy and vulnerable than going to bed with each other does. They are more wary of tenderness that goes with psychological and spiritual nakedness than of the physical nakedness in sexual intimacy."

One of the basic human hungerings is for tenderness and intimacy that will allow one to open up to another. Christ so loved us that He became vulnerable, He opened Himself up to us. To have a good relationship, this type of love is fundamental. If you dare to open yourself to another, you run the risk of being hurt. If you do not open up, there is no risk—just certainty that you and your relationship are not well.

Tenderness is the cutting edge of love. By tenderness, we are enabled to "Rejoice with them that do rejoice, and weep with them that weep" (Romans 12:15).

If you quit showing tenderness just because you feel pain, you will never know mature love and enjoy a fulfilling relationship. If we could read the secret history of our mate, we would find enough sorrow to solicit our fullest tenderness and disarm our hostility. There is no better exercise for the heart than to reach down tenderly and lift up another person.

Tenderness opens the door and lets in the estranged.

Tenderness is not always a sign of wisdom, but a lack of it reveals not one but several bad qualities, such as foolish vanity, indolence, ignorance, contempt for others, and jealousy. Tenderness, habitually practiced, gives greater charm to character than a display of great talent and dynamic drive. Nothing is lost and much is gained by tenderness. It is the cheapest of delights; it costs nothing and conveys much. Like mercy, it twice blesses, blessing the one who gives and the one who gets it.

What Joanne and Milt did for each other could have been done with resentment embellished by complaints. Their actions alone did not touch and motivate their friends to respond in kind. Their tenderness in little things with no selfish benefit in mind was the self-evident quality that influenced their circle of friends. Joanne did not just read to Milt—she read with feeling and an interpretive spirit. Milt did not just push Joanne's chair—he tenderly escorted her. The verbal and physical exchanges between them flowed from their hearts.

Syndicated columnist Ann Landers asked her readers whether they would be content to be held close and treated tenderly and forget about the act of sex. Approximately 72 percent said they would be content to be cuddled. Though the survey was a bit ambiguous, it was revealing. It was not clear in the survey as to whether the option was intended as an occasional alternative or a permanent one. Nevertheless, it dramatically stressed the importance of tenderness.

Dr. Joyce Brothers, in her syndicated column, noted this about Landers' survey, "I believe most women and men want and need tenderness as a part of love-making. . . . The 'how-to' books may not be stressing feelings and tenderness enough."

In her book *Sexual Choice*, anthropologist Heather Remoff deals with the thesis of the female's pursuit of a male. Though the word tenderness does not stand out on the pages of her works, it is a prominent theme interwoven throughout. She argues that the female stalks and captures the heart of aspiration. In her listing of the principle factors that make a male appealing and ignite the female's interest are words such as openness, sympathy, flexibility, honesty, understanding, and consideration. When totaled, those equal tenderness. If they are traits that attract a mate, they are characteristics that will help keep one and make life more enjoyable.

Though a macho image is often striking and initially appealing, it rapidly wanes. Most women opt for tenderness rather than a mere macho mentality. Machismo alone often indicates self-centeredness. When combined with tenderness, it is highly appealing.

Without Dissimulation

The kind of love that produces tenderness is further described in Romans 12 as being without dissimulation. *Dissimulation* is the word used to translate the Greek word *anupokritos*, which means to playact. Our word for it today is hypocrite. Hypocritical love is a contradiction in terms. If it is fake, it isn't love; if it is love, it isn't fake. Any attempt to fake love defrauds others and debilitates the actor.

In the Greek theater, one actor often played several roles. Each actor held a mask mounted on a short stick, each mask representing a different character. The same actor may appear later, using a different mask. Each mask was oversized and graphically depicted the intended character of the role being played. Actors who used such masks were called dissimulators. Against this background, the appeal in Romans 12 is for love to be real, not mere playacting.

A relationship based on playacting is a dramatic tragedy.

She was lovely, a Miss America with a plus. Her well-disciplined life-style was based on high moral standards. She was no play actress.

Wealth was but one of the assets of a handsome young doctor who entered her life through a spiritual portal.

They had been introduced by America's foremost evangelist of the era. He had been on the steering committee for the crusade. She had thrilled the crowd that filled the stadium with her heartfelt testimony. In her sharing, she spoke of how she never dated a nonchristian. She knew it was not right to be unequally yoked, therefore, she dated only men who were professing Christians. Her commitment was so strong that she did not want to take a chance of falling in love with the wrong person. She knew that if she never dated a person who wasn't her equal spiritually, she would never marry one.

Their meeting was spoken of as being made in heaven. Everything was so right. Miss America had met Mr. Wonderful. After a brief courtship, they were married. Why wait, when everything was so right?

Within six months, he laughed in her beautiful face, ridiculing her faith and mocking her ideals. Then came his stunning confession. It had seemed the social thing to do to get involved in the community effort related to the crusade. He knew of her beauty and had heard of her faith. On a bet, he set out to marry her. Now she couldn't believe what she was hearing. He admitted he knew all the right things to say and do to win her. Finally he said it: "I am not a Christian!"

His mask was off. She had been deceived by a playactor and trapped. The marriage lasted only a short time before dying an agonizing death. Theirs was an empty relationship based on deception.

Practicality if not integrity is a worthy motivation for keeping any single incident in your marriage from being based on hypocritical acting. If you never put on a mask, you never have to play the role. Fulfilling love is genuine, heartfelt.

Mask wearing wearies the wearer. Isolation and loneliness result. As long as the true you is hidden and not revealed, only the false you has fellowship and friendship. All the while the true you becomes more isolated and lonely as a result of having no one with which to relate. It is necessary to be true to yourself if you want true friendship.

Abhor That Which Is Evil

Love is a a two-edged sword: It has both a positive and negative blade. The positive side—that of genuine love—has been exposed. Now the negative: "Abhor that which is evil."

The Greek word for *abhor* comes from the Greek root *stugeto*, which means to hate. There are certain things that have no proper place in a marriage relationship. We should have abhorrence for them and rid ourselves of them. *Apo*, a preposition of ultimate source, is prefixed to the root. The ultimate source of evil is the mind. Mental sins are depicted as being worthy of our hate. This negates flirtation with ideas and attitudes that are wrong. Generously pour pre-emergent love on such seedbeds before they sprout and grow in your subconscious.

There is a saying that has been around so long that at least six sources are attributed with having originally stated it. The stream flows true, regardless of the fountain of its origin: "You can't keep the birds from flying over your head, but you can keep them from building their nest in your hair." Improper thoughts will occur to us. They are unavoidable. However, we can avoid giving mental assent to them. That is, we can disallow them as our desire. When an improper fantasy comes to mind, envision it as a vulture having come to make its habitat in your heart. If never given a branch on which to light, the fantasy's evil intent is driven away.

Ephesians 4:31, 32 speaks of some of these mental sins and clearly states what should be done with them: "Let all bitterness, and wrath, and anger, and clamour, and evil speaking, be put away from you, with all malice: And be ye kind one to another, tenderhearted, forgiving one another, even as God for Christ's sake hath forgiven you."

The first of these traits is even more directly attacked in Hebrews 12:15: "Looking diligently lest any man fail of the grace of God; lest any root of bitterness springing up trouble you, and thereby many be defiled."

If allowed, bitterness will hold a heart hostage. Contempt, not courtesy, should be shown bitterness; abhor it. Bitterness is selfishness; *agape* (love) is selfless. *Agape* penetrates the superficiality of momentary bitterness and gives itself. It is not based on the calculable value of another person to you, but on your nature.

Cleave to That Which Is Good

Cleave translates the Greek word *kollao*, which comes from the word for glue. Being in the present tense and middle voice, it means to keep on being united for your advantage. It is to your advantage to be mentally wed to that which is good. The good in reference is absolute good, divine good.

In the awakening hours of Creation, God said, "... It is not good that the man should be alone ..." (Genesis 2:18). God instituted marriage as being good. Our culture has dug up and reactivated every other form of cohabitation tried and found not to work by other cultures. Serial polygamy, communal living, and mere cohabiting have been tried by many former societies. In each instance, the verdict has been that none of them works as monogamous marriage does. Happily, a number of current studies reveal a return to monogamous marriage as the preferred life-style. Simple faith in God's Word would have prevented the pain associated with experimentation.

By memorizing portions of God's Word you can fix your mind on that which is good—even when conditions aren't. In crisis situations it can be recalled and application made. This can help avoid responding reflexively and unresponsibly to hostile treatment. Instead of reacting negatively, a positive response results. A preprogrammed mental attitude can result from meditating on God's Word. In this manner, internal control can be maintained, regardless of what painful complexity swirls around you. When a story of controversy is brewing, a good attitude can be maintained. By sticking to this strategy, love (*agape*) will prevail, even if for a while it appears not to be working. If a believer lays down the weapons provided by God for spiritual warfare and takes up the weapons of the opponent, a loss is certain. Persons not committed to the concepts of Christ are more adept and experienced than Christians in using weapons of the world. Stick to your guns.

Be Kindly Affectioned

A practical application of this principle deserves consideration. We are urged in Romans 12:10 "Be kindly affectioned one to another with brotherly love...." Kindly affectioned translates an adjective used regarding mutual love of a parent and child. Natural affection comes from natural birth. Elevated to a spiritual plane, one who experiences new birth should show affection for others. Reliance upon the supernatural source enables this trait to prevail. It is an inward attitude resulting in an outward action.

Such affection becomes a passionate desire of the mind. It prompts kindness and friendliness regardless of what suffering is imposed. In the case of harsh and unfair treatment being inflicted on a marriage partner, this trait may seem unreasonable, yet it is the only practical and productive response possible. By determining that this will be a characteristic of yours, regardless of how dirty another person may fight, you have a winnable game plan. It may not always work, but nothing else will. All alternatives have been tried and found futile.

Take a giant step to a better relationship. Resolve: "I *will* be kindly affectioned. I will always be kind and friendly." If you make this commitment, expect to be tested. Joy is inherent in passing the test.

With Brotherly Love

Brotherly love is a part of being kindly affectioned. This is a command to be devoted. Devotion will be tested daily—expect that. Without brotherly love, no marriage or business relationship can last. No couple has ever remained true to each other simply because there was no opportunity to be unfaithful. Wave after assault wave can be expected on your relationship. Only a mind set of devotion can enable it to withstand the siege. Anticipation of the thrill of victory strengthens devotion. Consider it a challenging delight to maintain your devotion—value it. A lack of devotion by your mate in some instance should not cause you to want to respond in kind. Such action-reaction tears you further apart. A lack of devotion by your partner is an occasion to prove yours. Devotion encourages devotion.

John, a respected churchman for many years, had all the superficial appearances of being a good family man. But when the veneer of his life was peeled away, a dark underside was exposed. Repetitious promiscuous relations, incest, and child abuse dotted his past.

Mary, his devoted wife, had lived for years as a betrayed wife. Traumatized at first, she lived with a broken heart during John's prison sentence. The wolf of want slept on her doorstep during his years of imprisonment. She sought psychological and spiritual help for him and waited. Her middle-aged beauty and apparent vulnerability made her the object of many overtures by would-be lovers. One trait characterized her—devotion. It became increasingly apparent that she really meant it when she pledged her love for better or worse. This was the worst at its worst. She is still waiting, and the courts indicate her vigil will be long. Her ambition is the rehabilitation of her beloved.

Preferring One Another

As you consider the tests of your devotion, remember Mary's example. It is not dissimilar to that shown by Christ for His bride, the Church. This devotion results in a couple "in honour preferring one another." To honor means to recognize merit and show appreciation. It is evidenced when a person looks for and acknowledges admirable acts and shows appreciation for little things as well as major ones. Recall from your childhood the magic words "please" and "thank you." They should be an accent revealing speech that comes from a heart of love. They should betray a kind and gentle heart.

By being observant of things to compliment, you will have occasion to brag about your mate privately and publicly. Those who show affection and shower attention on each other are multiply blessed. Even if you don't get your share, be certain you give more than your share. By doing so, you are teaching your partner that these are things you like. Also, it shows him that this is treatment you would not mind receiving.

Having dealt with horizontal fellowship, now the inspired penman gives insight regarding our vertical love. They are both interrelated.

Not Slothful in Business

"Not slothful in business" is an expression related to professional conduct. Ambition and personal pride cause people to want to be their best in their vocation. The appeal not to be slothful literally means don't be slow and pokey at your job. Such behavior betrays a divided mind, a major distraction present in your life. It might well be interpreted as a significant sign that you do not have the right attitude toward someone or something.

Research by Dr. Heather Remoff revealed some of the traits that attract a woman are good income potential, control of material resources, a good provider, and aggressiveness. Financial security is basic security in marriage. When a partner feels financially insecure or uncertain, fear comes into play. This lack of confidence and assurance causes instability, which ultimately results in a loss of confidence.

Both partners in a relationship need to know their total financial picture. If it is good, they can work together to utilize it wisely. If it is bad, they can unite to adjust and compensate. Uncertainty is discomforting.

Even if the financial picture isn't good, but it is apparent that a conscientious effort is being made, there is encouragement and hope. No amount of money has ever assured stability in marriage. It is not the amount that matters; it is the attitude toward it that counts.

When a person is not performing to the optimum, there is usually a deep personal awareness. No one can enjoy self-acceptance while having a guilt complex resulting from goofing off. Only a sense of having done a job well gives a good self-image. A poor self-image results in a defensive approach to relationships. A resolute determination to be involved and productive in work shows concern. A will to succeed says, "I care and want to help provide for you."

Fervent in Spirit

"Fervent in spirit" is the next appeal. *Zeo* is the Greek word for fervent. It literally means to be boiling—an expression used for zealous. This boiling zeal comes from the Holy Spirit, but it should be the nature of your spirit. No one likes to be around a negative, depressed, unenergetic person. Most prefer to associate with vivacious individuals whose very being is refreshing.

Kathy is a prime example. The place where she worked experienced a 20 percent increase in business because of her. She was life with a plus. Her high energy level, warm, friendly smile, and dynamic demeanor raised the energy flow of all around her. She not only did her job with zest but by example inspired her fellow workers. Customers came in just to be uplifted by her. On occasion I took people with a "downer disposition" in, just to watch her influence on them. Invariably they left with a glow. That which works in business works even better in marriage. Pizzazz is a quiet picker-upper.

Action-reaction: It works both ways. Positive action can build a relationship. Negative reaction can kill not only the will of the one acting, but the relationship as well. It is not strength of personality that prevails, but resolute determination to persevere.

Have you ever attended an athletic event, perhaps a basketball game, where the crowd responded enthusiastically and the players played better? As the players perform better, the crowd becomes more vocal.

This is seen in some churches where the congregation responds to the preacher and he becomes more animated and assertive. As he does, they react even more expressively.

In these instances there is a great circle of energy flowing. Ideally a husband-wife or parent-child relationship needs this circle of energy. Someone has to start it. Frequently, more time than imagined is needed to get the flow started. The one who resolves to start it must expect discouragement but resolve not to stop the effort.

Conversely, a lack of energy drains energy. For this reason a negative action-reaction relationship has nowhere to go but down.

Some people seem to think cheerfulness and enthusiasm just happen to some people. Nothing is further from the truth. Few things are more challenging than learning to be excited about what you are doing every day. There is work in learning to be excited about your work and relationships every day. Failure to be fervent in spirit today makes tomorrow even more difficult. Zeal can turn a zero into a person charged with zest. Many make the mistake of leaving their zeal at their place of employment; wise people bring it into their relationships at home.

Serving the Lord

Next in the text is a matchless mental motivator. Make this a bumper sticker for your brain: "Serving the Lord." Envision yourself as employed by the Lord for the purpose of putting together a good relationship. Complaining about the products you have to work with does no good. Take what you have and make do. Stories abound of successful people who became productive with great limitations.

Sir Walter Scott and Lord Byron had many things in common. Both hobbled through life on clubbed feet. They are not known for this, but as gallant models of gentlemanliness, grace, and refinement. John Milton's powerful pen produced *Paradise Lost* even though he was blind.

Perhaps your partner in a relationship is your greatest handicap. That should stimulate and challenge you, rather than defeat you. Let building a good relationship be a task assigned you by the Lord. Thus, He is seen as the one for whom you are working on the assignment. He is the one to whom you must answer. Be loyal to Him by being faithful to your task of relationship building. The more difficult the task, the greater the confidence He has shown in you.

God alone will grade your finals. Regardless of how others react to your service, live in such a way as to eventually garner His "Well done, thou good and faithful servant."

Elevate your attitude about every task. When cleaning the kitchen you are not just washing dishes—you are serving the Lord. You are not merely showing common courtesy when offended—you are serving the Lord. You are not only being polite when you bless those who curse you—you are serving the Lord. Serve the Lord with gladness. When you do, those around you will take note. Don't ask to read their notes, but be assured they will show them to others.

Rejoicing in Hope

All the while we are serving the Lord we are to be "rejoicing in hope." Our hope is in Jesus Christ alone. Those who live in the sphere of hope tinged with joy are sustained thereby. Our word *hope* came from a combination of two old Anglo-Saxon word meanings. The words were the equivalent of our words desire and expectation. When you desire to achieve a certain end, you are motivated to work for it. When you expect to reach the desired end, momentum is given the effort.

Do you desire to have a good relationship with your partner? If not, you need to renew your mind. To do this, remember how it began. It was once good, even fun. It can never be that good again—it can, however, be *better* than it ever was. Your marriage can be made stronger through struggle.

Do you expect to have a good relationship? What do you expect out of your partner? Most people have an indirect way of telegraphing their expectations. When disappointed, code words such as, "Well, what did you expect?" are used. A good "Well, I thought so," can go a long way toward deflating a person. When there is a failure, "I knew it," confirms a low expectation.

There are positive signals to communicate positive expectations, also. Wisdom encourages that they be learned and used often. Some are: "I'm proud of you." "You did well." "I like that, you should do that more often." An all-time classic that stands alone is a simple "Thanks."

Hope makes the next trait possible.

Patient in Tribulation

We are to be "patient in tribulation." Patience is not merely passive endurance; it is active perseverance. It is the courage to carry on against all odds and obstacles. Confidence in a cause makes one patient in trying to achieve it. Patience is a renewable resource. Patience keeps hope alive, and hope gives endurance to patience.

Tribulation is translated from the Greek word *thlipsis*, meaning "affliction." Tribulation is trouble gone manic. The word was used to describe a person reclining with a large stone on his chest. You simply have to be patient with stones.

Patience enables one to wait for the Lord to enable the removal of such a weight.

Continuing Instant in Prayer

Only a patient person will progress to the next step of "continuing instant in prayer." Here we find the supernatural ingredient needed for a good marital bond. Hope and patience enable one to wait expectantly for the Lord to answer prayer. Give God time to be God—don't rush Him. Often a time lapse between the request and the answer is allowed in order to draw you closer to the Lord. If so, that will do you as much good as an immediate direct answer.

Many people substitute counterfeits for prayer. Some substitute good works accompanied by the motto: "God helps those who help themselves." Actually God helps the helpless. Others substitute conversation for prayer. They talk more with people about their problem than they do with God. This is a misleading dodge. Discussion relieves tension but rarely solves a problem unless it is with the one involved. A third replacement for prayer is therapy. Much money is spent on this alternative.

Why pray?

    1. By prayer you participate in a divine activity.
    2. It is an act of taking sides with God and admitting you want what He wants.
    3. It is an affirmation of concern for others.
    4. It is a declaration of dependence on God.

This simple verse contrasts the options:

> "The devil trembles when he sees,
> The weakest Christian on his knees."

Now the counterpoint . . .

> "The devil glories when he views,
> The strongest Christian with the blues."

Prayer should not be your last resort—it should be your first resource.

A broader sphere of responsibility for resources at your disposal now comes into focus in Romans 12:13-16. Each principle is a couplet dealing with both sides of issues. As you inventory them, resolve to develop the positive aspects as personal traits.

Distributing to the Necessity of Saints

We are to be engaged in "distributing to the necessity of saints." *Koinoneo* is the Greek word translated "distributing." It is a word for sharing or fellowship. In this text, it speaks of helping others in a time of need. Wisdom reveals this to be therapeutic. By broadening our interests and concerns, we avoid becoming introverted and excessively introspective. It is paradoxical that a way to lighten your own burden is to help others with theirs.

Given to Hospitality

The flip side encourages us to be "given to hospitality." This appeals for us to make people feel at home around us. Are people comfortable in your presence? We can unconsciously develop traits that make people feel uncomfortable around us.

Ask yourself this hard question: "Am I fun to live with?" Don't kid yourself. If the honest answer is no, something can be done about it. Begin by evaluating how you can open your heart and become more hospitable. What traits can and should you develop? In deciding whether you want to or not, pause and reflect on how you felt the last time you were with someone who had this ability. Super-good, wasn't it? Now you have the picture. That is the way you can make people feel around you. Unofficially and informally host the person to whom you relate. It makes two people feel good—the other person and you.

Bless Them Which Persecute You

Are you sure, really sure, you want a better relationship? If you do, you must "bless them which persecute you." This is the acid test. An associated couplet goes with this, "bless, and curse not."

"Bless" translates the Greek word *eulogeo*. In its pronunciation can be heard our word eulogy. It means to speak well of, to eulogize. Regardless of how others speak of us, we are to speak well of them. We are not responsible for their attitudes or opinions. We are accountable for ours. No amount of negativism should be allowed to erode our lofty opinion of another person. This does not imply being unaware of their actions; it simply means you are bigger than they. We do not think well of others because they deserve it, but because our nature demands it.

Curse Not

"Curse not" means don't run them down. By employing this technique, rapport can be maintained even when there is antagonism on one person's behalf. If you are inclined to call down curses on those who disagree with or oppose you, forget it. A tit-for-tat relationship is a sick one.

People spiritually mature enough to treat abrasive persons in this way will surely be able to show their beloved the same consideration. An aggressive way to apply this is to look for ways to show appreciation and express encouragement. You never build up yourself by tearing down others. Relationships are built by building up people.

Rejoice With Them . . . .

A progressive step is suggested next in the text: "Rejoice with them that do rejoice, and weep with them that weep."

In a word, empathize. In two words, be thoughtful. To do so is to share another's feelings, to be attentive to moods.

No person is always in the same mood. Mood swings need to be studied. When you love a person, you will be alert to mood swings. This requires selflessness. It requires being more attentive to another person than to yourself, and we are not prone to do this naturally. Our natural instinct is to want others to be sensitive to our feelings. Anyone who waits for such favorable treatment is likely to be disappointed. This is not true simply because others are not likely to consider your feelings. This attitude reveals such selfishness that it can't be satisfied.

Shakespeare, in his work *As You Like It*, gave us an illustration. Brothers were both in love. One succeeded in his courtship. The other, having failed, exclaimed: "How bitter it is to look into happiness through another's eyes!" Having failed in love, he also failed in attitude by not entering into the joy of another. Thoughtful people are baptized into the feelings of others.

Be of the Same Mind

Following this appeal for emotional togetherness comes an encouragement to share a mutual mental attitude: "Be of the same mind one toward another. Mind not high things, but condescend to men of low estate. Be not wise in your own conceits" (Romans 12:16).

It is hard to love another person from the top of a one-person pedestal. Those willing to come down and identify with menial tasks and humble people will find people relate to them warmly. A servant temperament works to a person's advantage in all areas of life, but never more so than in a marital relationship.

This paragraph is likely to be one of the few you ever read that advocates such a temperament. Most best-sellers advocate the opposite. Numero Uno is always to be considered first, according to the world's standard. A pictoral summary of the attitude advocated by most best-sellers would depict a person climbing a ladder. While stomping the hands of those on the ladder beneath them, they are licking the boots of those above them. There is no room in a marriage for a prima donna. Most ads appeal to a self-pampering, overly self-indulgent personality. In doing so, they are indirectly endorsing and encouraging such a self-preening personality.

In contrast to this is the person who gets great gratification out of doing for others. Often the deeds are done in secret. This reveals that the reward is in the doing, not in praise or accolades. A lady in Philadelphia who has become known as "the meter beater" is a good example. By cutting out soft drinks she saves enough money to put coins in parking meters that are about to expire. This saves the police from having to write a ticket and the car owner the expense and inconvenience of having to pay a fine. Rarely does anyone see her do it. She is not reimbursed and never thanked. When asked why she did it, she simply replied, "I know I do it, and it makes me feel good." That is a prime reason for doing whatever we do. If the reward is in the doing, then do what is right and don't dare stop, even if appreciation is never acknowledged. Inherent in the deed is the delight—do it.

Every relationship experiences hardship.

Problems can either be a blessing or a burden. They can bond you together or blast you apart—it all depends on your response. How we respond to what happens to us is more important than what happens to us, since we can't determine what happens to us, but we can determine our response.

The next five verses of Romans 12 give us the practical means of applying a strategic principle. The principle is this: Never let a problem cause you to attack each other. Always let a problem cause you two to unite and attack the problem together. When considered in this light, even a problem becomes a blessing.

If your partner does not fulfill his or her role in your relationship, don't forfeit yours. Just as two wrongs don't make a right, so two who are wrong have more trouble getting right.

If you conduct yourself properly and your partner responds correctly, you will have no need to change. You will already be in character. By maintaining proper conduct at all times you model proper conduct and are thus likely to motivate kindred responses. Even if this doesn't happen, you will have the consolation of knowing you have done the right thing. That is fulfilling.

Recompense to No Man Evil for Evil

A peerless passage on how to respond amid hardships is recorded in Romans 12:17–21. It begins by advocating that we "Recompense to no man evil for evil. Provide things honest in the sight of all men." Anyone who dares to do this exercises influence more profound, more extensive, more enduring, and more eventful than he can imagine.

The sun will rise in the west before two wrongs make a right. When a person is allowed to control your reaction, rather than Christ controlling your action, then you have permitted that person to be your master. Play the mental game, "Who is in control here?" Ask yourself, "Will I let this person make a marionette of me and dance on his or her strings?" When we automatically respond in kind to one who has done us an injustice, we have condescended to the role of his puppet.

Provide Things Honest

We are at all times to "provide things honest." Poet Robert Burns noted, "An honest man's the noblest work of God." To allow our Creator to exercise His craftsmanship, we must conclude with Milton, "I am resolved to live and die an honest man."

Such integrity should be displayed "in the sight of all men." A jewel should be mounted in such a way that its beauty meets the eye. When virtue and honesty are displayed consistently, they garner admiration and solicit like response.

Live Peaceably

"If it be possible, as much as lieth in you, live peaceably with all men." This is an appeal never to let the cause of conflict come from within you.

"Peaceably" speaks of harmony. There are two qualifications related to this quality. They are: If it be possible, and as far as depends on you.

Unfortunately it is not always possible, but insofar as it is, be sure all depending on you makes it possible. Avoid being the cause of conflict; always be the cure. This can be done by maintaining an inward harmony awaiting an opportunity to share in concert with your partner. If you do this, you will be a friend of Christ, conqueror of the world, and heir of heaven.

We can't avoid conflict. We can avoid conflict caused by not following the will of God. Some persons are so out of God's will that you will automatically be in conflict with them. If you are to have conflict, make sure it is with a purpose. Make sure it is because you are in God's will and not out of it. When aligned with His will, you can be assured of His blessings when in a conflict caused by obedience to Him. In such conflict He becomes your companion.

Avenge Not

"Avenge not yourselves . . . Vengeance is mine; I will repay, saith the Lord." To do this, you must "give place to wrath." When we avenge ourselves we rob God of the right. Vengeance rightfully belongs to the Lord, who does it far more effectively. His vengeance is not revenge, it is simply the law of His preannounced wrath in operation. God is no bungler. Those who trust Him to take care of the situation spare themselves unnecessary efforts. There is no guarantee of immediate vindication, however you can be assured He will accomplish it in due time. If you have aligned yourself with His cause, it is inevitable, because He defends His cause. Those associated with it have the good fortune of the same protection it gets.

If Thine Enemy Hunger. . . .

"Therefore if thine enemy hunger, feed him; if he thirst, give him drink: for in so doing thou shalt heap coals of fire on his head."

When you conduct yourself properly and speak kindly, there is a commendable consequence. "Burning coals" is interpreted by some to be a reference to burning pangs of shame and contrition. Perhaps! However, there is a positive way in which this is achieved. In antiquity only the wealthy could afford fire. It was almost a luxury. After the benevolent wealthy had used their fires, the poor were allowed to collect some of the coals for their use. They were put in a container and, as was the custom, carried on the head. Thus, the coals were a blessing. This passage teaches that when you provide the needs of one in an adversary position you are blessing him. This blessing puts him to shame, and this results in burning pangs of shame and contrition.

Be Not Overcome of Evil

"Be not overcome of evil, but overcome evil with good."

This is a summary of all that has been said. It is essential to developing a better relationship.

"Overcome" translates the Greek word *nikao*. It was a word for conquest. The literal interpretation would be, "Don't be conquered by evil, but conquer evil by surrounding it with good." Siege should be laid against evil attitudes and actions. Surround them and overwhelm them with good. A worldly philosophy would advocate retaliation. To give kindness and express love when not deserved and least called for can win an adversary—even your mate. When it does, you have built a better relationship.

Here is a means to that end. First, memorize this entire passage of Scripture. In addition to being a good mental exercise, it will program your mind and enable the verse to be incorporated into your personality. Repeat it to yourself at least once a day in order to keep it fresh. When an experience occurs that you recognize as one of the negatives described herein, think of the counterpoint offered in God's Word. Upon realizing this, silently pray for strength to respond in the scriptural manner. This will make you an ambassador of God's love.

When the conflict ends, stop and assess your response and the result. Think of how you will respond the next time you are confronted with a similar situation. If you have experienced victory, take time to thank God and arm yourself for the next confrontation. Expect it! If you have suffered defeat, thank the Lord for the joy of engaging in conflict according to His standard. Ask Him to help you be found faithful in all future conflicts, regardless of the outcome.

Pause now and read the entire Bible passage (Romans 12:9–21). Do you agree that it is good strategy? If so, will you commit yourself to using it? Try it. You have the power of heaven on your side when you do. Take the first step toward a better relationship, learn the stepping-stones through the marriage marsh.

11

Got a Problem?
Got Five Minutes?
Read This!

Y ou are a special person.
    Nobody can take your place.
        Everybody needs somebody.
            The wisest person needs counsel
                Sometimes about something.

A high school student wrote a paper on Socrates that was brief and on target. "Socrates," he wrote, "was a Greek philosopher who went around giving advice. They poisoned him."

Maybe you don't want advice. Maybe you have "poisoned" all would-be givers of advice by turning them off or cutting them up. Why?

Ancient Paduan theologians refused to look through the newly invented telescope. Their reason? They were afraid they would see something they could not believe.

Are you afraid to listen to advice from any person or receive it from any source? If so, why?

Please don't stop reading. The answer to that question may open a doorway to the solution of many of your problems.

First, admit it—you have a problem. You would not have read this far if you didn't have one and were not conscientiously interested in doing something about it. Say it out loud: "I have a problem." Say it again. This time emphasize the first word: "*I* have a problem." This problem may involve other people and have a number of complex parts, but by admitting whose problem it is, you have a starting point.

Why have you been afraid to look through the telescope? There is a reason. Check to see if one of these is yours.

>   1. I have my mind made up, and I am afraid logic will prove I am wrong. (If this is true, it is a silent self-admission that you suspect you are wrong.)
>
>   2. I am tired of trying, and new insight might inspire me to continue the struggle. (If this is true, you have a secret hope that a solution can be found. With the insight will come the inspiration to carry on, if you will only open yourself to counsel.)
>
>   3. I might have to admit my error. (If so, this will prove how big you are and draw others to you for acting responsibly.)
>
>   4. I will have to adjust my life. (Adjustment can be good. Change can bring even more happiness.)

All of us have areas we are afraid to explore. You might just be wise enough to identify and admit yours. If you have, *congratulations.*

Forget about your problem for a moment. Instead, identify

the need in your relationship that has caused the problem. What is the *need*?

Having identified the need, now propose a solution. What is the means to help fulfill the need? Be specific in proposing the solution. Make sure the solution is one that will maintain your relationship. Breaking it isn't a good solution. That may be mere avoidance.

Now resolve to put the solution into action. Do it!

Review the steps: identify the need; propose the solution; put it into practice.

Recapitulate what has been said so far. Get it clear. If you have a problem:

Admit it candidly.
   Identify it openly.
      Discuss it honestly.
         Analyze it carefully.
            Resolve it lovingly.

Married couples have spent much time and money on each other—don't waste your investment of time and effort. If you are contemplating breaking your marriage relationship and starting another one, try this instead. Take the money you will have to spend in order to establish another relationship and spend it on your present partner. If it would impress another person, it will impress your mate. Use the time you plan to spend with another person just as constructively with your spouse. All of this will take less time and cost less than a divorce.

Admit your part of the problem and concede there is a solution.

The wise men of law in Jerusalem believed the Messiah would be born in Bethlehem. However, they would not walk ten miles to see if He had been born—belief must be followed by action.

Resolve to be teachable. Truthfully evaluate whether or not one of these adjectives fits you: obstinate, bullheaded, stubborn, belligerent, or cantankerous.

Don't wait too long. The fact that you have read this far indicates it isn't too late to save your marriage.

After a stimulating hour of counsel, the husband looked at his watch and abruptly said, "We've got to go at once." I asked for five minutes to conclude. He insisted they didn't have five minutes, explaining that their final divorce hearing was coming up in thirty minutes. If they had been willing to work at restoring their relationship, it would not have been too late for them.

Kathleen and Dave had not waited too long, even though they had been divorced for six months. It was unfortunate that they did not come to a more sensible decision a few months earlier, but even after their divorce they both realized their error, sought counsel, and applied it. They are now happily remarried to each other.

In order to avoid waiting too long, don't wait any longer—act now.

My friend Charlie "Tremendous" Jones is noted for this brilliant observation: *Nothing works.*

Nothing works, but you must. If you work at it, your relationship will work.

Everybody needs help at some time in some way. Auto mechanics make a living because people need help with their cars. Transportation companies exist because people need help. Lawyers stay in business because people need help. The fact that you need help with your relationship simply identifies you with humanity.

Seek help. Find a source of godly counsel. Make sure this is a competent source you can trust. Don't look for one you think will tell you what you want to hear. Obtain a source of professional counsel who will tell you what you need to hear. Go immediately, listen carefully to what is said, and make mental application at the moment. This will enable you to put into practice what is shared.

Seek a single source of competent counsel and stick with the one chosen. Don't run from one to another. By all means stay away from friends who have messed up their own lives and now feel competent to counsel you on how to foul up your own.

Nothing works—you must. Try these first steps.

Compliment your spouse. Help with a chore that is not normally yours. Engage in conversation on a topic of interest to your spouse. Improve your grooming, make yourself attractive. Break a bad habit. Encourage your spouse. Worship together often and regularly.

Those are good starters. It will amaze you how good you will feel and how much better your relationship will become if you use them. It only takes a spark to get a fire started.

"To profit from good advice requires more wisdom than to give it," said philosopher John Collins.

Note this fact: It never helps to slam the door.

What It Will Cost You to Call It Quits

In considering a divorce, most people consider two things:
Costs: "Can I afford it?"
Ease: "What personal relief will I get?"

Following are other things to consider, listed in simple terms without details, in order that they might be more easily digested. Consider these ramifications of a divorce.

Fear   Relational fears will develop.
Trust will diminish.
Suspicion of the opposite sex grows.
What will the children think?
How will this affect the children's future?
Will relatives on either or both sides reject me?

Guilt   Personal questions will linger.
Was it my fault—at least in part?
What have I done to my children?
How do I stand with God?

Anger   Anger and frustration become complex.
Will a root of bitterness control my thoughts?

Will this experience rob me of joy?
Will resentment color all of my life?

Self-worth Feelings of rejection, unworthiness, and defeat.
A sense of disappointment, cruelty, and unworthiness.

Finances Fees for lawyers, court, and settlement.
Moving expenses.
Possible loss of credit and inability to qualify for a loan.
Lower standard of living in general.

Parenting Parenting becomes a process of negotiation.
Children become messengers and/or tattletales between parents.
Consistency between ex-mates in rearing children is a problem.

Most divorces result in exchanging one set of problems for all the above, plus many unknown problems. In many cases it would be much easier to work out the problems suggesting a divorce rather than confronting this new complexity. A sense of dignity and pride results from building a stronger relationship with your present partner.